Air Fryer Oven Cookbook For Beginners

Air Fryer Recipes For Beginners, Learn About An Air Fryer With Amazingly Around 200 Tasty Recipes to Fry, Roast, Grill, & Bake With Your Air Fryer & 1500 Days Meal Plan.

By

Marc Williamson

© **Copyright 2022 by Marc Williamson - All rights reserved.**

This document is geared towards providing exact and reliable information regarding the topic and issue covered. The publication is sold with the idea that the publisher is not required to render accounting, officially permitted, or otherwise, qualified services. If advice is necessary, legal or professional, a practiced individual in the profession should be ordered.

- From a Declaration of Principles, which was accepted and approved equally by a Committee of the American Bar Association and a Committee of Publishers and Associations.

In no way is it legal to reproduce, duplicate, or transmit any part of this document in either electronic means or in printed format. Recording of this publication is strictly prohibited, and any storage of this document is not allowed unless with written permission from the publisher. All rights reserved.

The information provided herein is stated to be truthful and consistent, in that any liability, in terms of inattention or otherwise, by any usage or abuse of any policies, processes, or directions contained within is the solitary and utter responsibility of the recipient reader. Under no circumstances will any legal responsibility or blame be held against the publisher for any reparation, damages, or monetary loss due to the information herein, either directly or indirectly.

Respective authors own all copyrights not held by the publisher.

The information herein is offered for informational purposes solely and is universal as so. The presentation of the information is without a contract or any type of guaranteed assurance.

The trademarks that are used are without any consent, and the publication of the trademark is without permission or backing by the trademark owner. All trademarks and brands within this book are for clarifying purposes only and are owned by the owners themselves, not affiliated with this document.

Table of contents

Introduction 10
Chapter 1: What Is An Air Fryer? 11
    1.1 Working Mechanism of Air Fryer 11
    1.2 What could you cook in the air fryer? 11
    1.3 How to clean the Air Fryer? 12
4-Week Meal Plan 13
    Week 1 13
    Week 2 14
    Week 3 15
    Week 4 16
Chapter 2: Appetizer Recipes 17
    2.1   Air Fryer Pickles 17
    2.2   Air Fryer Crispy Sriracha Spring Rolls 17
    2.3   Air Fryer Fiesta Chicken Fingers 18
    2.4   Air Fryer Cheeseburger Onion Rings 19
    2.5   Garlic Rosemary Sprouts 20
    2.6   Air Fryer Ravioli 20
    2.7   Air Fryer Taquitos 21
    2.8   Air Fryer General Tso's Cauliflower 22
    2.9   Air Fryer Nashville Hot Chicken 23
    2.10   Air Fryer Pumpkin Fries 23
    2.11   Sweet & Spicy Air Fryer Meatballs 24
    2.12   Air Fryer Ham & Cheese Turnovers 25
    2.13   Air Fryer Pepper Poppers 25
    2.14   Air Fryer Wasabi Crab Cakes 26
    2.15   Air Fryer Caribbean Wontons 27
    2.16   Air fryer Beefy Swiss Bundles 28
    2.17   Air Fryer Tortellini with Prosciutto 29
    2.18   Air Fryer Crispy Curry Drumsticks 30
    2.19   Air Fryer Rosemary Sausage Meatballs 30
    2.20   Air Fryer Egg Rolls 31
    2.21   Air Fryer Turkey Croquettes 32

2.22	Air Fryer Cauliflower Tots	32
2.23	Spicy Pickle Fries (Dill)	33
2.24	Stuffed Mushroom with Sour Cream	33
2.25	Honey Sriracha Air Fryer Wings	34
2.26	Air Fryer Buffalo Ranch Chickpeas	35
2.27	Air Fryer Sweet Potato Tots	35
2.28	Air Fryer Korean Chicken Wings	36
2.29	Air Fried Mozzarella Sticks	37
2.30	Air Fryer Pakoras	38
2.31	Bacon Wrapped Scallops along with Sriracha Mayo	38
2.32	Air Fryer Balsamic Glazed Chicken Wings	39
2.33	Air Fryer Loaded Greek Fries	40
2.34	Air Fryer Arancini	41
2.35	Air Fryer Mac & Cheese Ball	42
2.36	Air Fryer Fingerling Potatoes with Dip	43
2.37	Air Fryer Taco Soup	43
2.38	Air Fryer Coconut Shrimp	44
2.39	Air Fryer Loaded Cheese & Onion Fries	45
2.40	Air Fryer Paneer Pakoras	46
2.41	Air Fryer Pork Balls	47
2.42	Air Fryer Crab Cake	47
2.43	Homemade Chicharrones, Pork Rind	48

Chapter 3: Breakfast Recipes		**50**
3.1	Air Fryer Apple Fritters	50
3.2	Air Fryer French Toast Sticks	51
3.3	Air Fryer Breakfast Toad-in-the-Hole Tarts	51
3.4	Air Fryer Churros	52
3.5	Air Fryer Hard Boiled Eggs	53
3.6	Air Fryer Omelet	53
3.7	Air Fryer McDonald's Copycat Egg McMuffin	54
3.8	Air Fryer Breakfast Pizza	54
3.9	Air Fryer Cherry and Cream Cheese Danish	55
3.10	Air-Fryer Southern Cheese	55
3.11	Air-Fried Breakfast Bombs	56
3.12	Air Fryer Biscuit Breakfast Bombs	56

3.13	Air Fryer Stuffed Breakfast Bombs with Eggs & Bacon	58
3.14	Air Fryer Breakfast Burritos	58
3.15	Air Fryer Breakfast Frittata	59
3.16	Air Fryer Crispy Bacon	59
3.17	Air Fryer Raspberry Muffins	59
3.18	Air Fryer Tofu	60
3.19	Air Fryer Brussel Sprouts	60

Chapter 4: Lunch Recipes 62

4.1	Air Fryer Donuts	62
4.2	Bang Bang Chicken	63
4.3	Crispy Air Fryer Eggplant Parmesan	64
4.4	Air Fryer Shrimp Fajitas	65
4.5	Honey Glazed Air Fryer Salmon	65
4.6	Crispy Air Fryer Roasted Brussels Sprouts With Balsamic	66
4.7	Air Fryer Chicken Nuggets	67
4.8	Air Fryer Baked Apples	67
4.9	Air Fryer Fish Tacos	68
4.10	Air Fryer Dumplings	68
4.11	Air Fryer Pork Special Chops	69
4.12	Air Fryer Chicken Chimichangas	70
4.13	Simple Chicken Burrito Bowls	70
4.14	Chicken Soft Tacos	71
4.15	Ground Pork Tacos - Al Pastor Style	72
4.16	Air-Fryer Southern-Style Chicken	73
4.17	Air-Fryer Fish & Fries	73
4.18	Air-Fryer Ground Beef Wellington	74
4.19	Air-Fryer Stylish Ravioli	75
4.20	Popcorn Shrimp Tacos with Cabbage Slaw	76
4.21	Bacon-Wrapped Avocado Wedges	77
4.22	Air-Fryer Steak Fajitas	77
4.23	Air-Fryer Sweet & Sour Pork	78
4.24	Air-Fryer Taco Twists	79
4.25	Air-Fryer Potato Chips	79
4.26	Air-Fryer Greek Breadsticks	80
4.27	Air-Fryer Crumb-Topped Sole	80

4.28	Air-Fried Radishes	81
4.29	Air-Fryer Ham & Egg Pockets	81
4.30	Air-Fryer Eggplant Fries	82
4.31	Air-Fryer Turkey Croquettes	82
4.32	Garlic-Herb Fried Patty Pan Squash	83
4.33	Air-Fryer Quinoa Arancini	84
4.34	Air-Fryer General Tso's Cauliflower	84
4.35	Air-Fryer Pork Chops	85
4.36	Air-Fryer Nacho Hot Dogs	86
4.37	Air-Fryer Raspberry Balsamic Smoked Pork Chops	86
4.38	Air-Fryer Chickpea Fritters with Sweet-Spicy Sauce	87
4.39	Air-Fryer Crispy Sriracha Spring Rolls	88
4.40	Air-Fryer Pork Schnitzel	89
4.41	Air-Fryer Green Tomato Stacks	90
4.42	Air-Fryer Pretzel-Crusted Catfish	90
4.43	Air-Fryer French Toast Cups with Raspberries	91
4.44	Air Fryer Ham & Cheese Turnovers	92
4.45	Air-Fryer Shrimp Po'boys	92
4.46	Air-Fryer Papas Rellenas	93
4.47	Air-Fryer Herb & Cheese-Stuffed Burgers	94
4.48	Nashville Hot Special Chicken	95
4.49	Air-Fryer Salmon with Maple-Dijon Glaze	95
4.50	Air Fryer Tortellini with Prosciutto	96
4.51	Air-Fryer Cumin Carrots	97
4.52	Air-Fryer Mini Chimichangas	97
4.53	Air-Fryer Fiesta Chicken Fingers	98
4.54	Air-Fryer Everything Bagel Chicken Strips	99
4.55	Air-Fryer Peach-Bourbon Wings	99
4.56	Turkey Breast Tenderloins in the Air Fryer	100
4.57	Air Fryer Rotisserie Roasted Whole Chicken	101

Chapter 5: Dinner Recipes 102

5.1	Air Fryer Shrimp	102
5.2 Air Fryer Loaded Pork Burritos		102
5.3 Air Fryer Sweet & Sour Pineapple Pork		104
5.4 Air Fryer Green Tomato BLT		104

5.5 Air fryer roasted green beans 105

5.6 Air fryer spicy chicken breasts.. 106

5.7 Air fryer Reuben Calzones 106

5.8 Teriyaki Salmon Fillets with Broccoli 107

5.9 Air fryer steak with garlic herb butter 108

5.10 Air fryer fried rice with sesame sriracha sauce 108

5.11 Air fryer Roast Chicken 109

5.12 Air Fryer Mini Swedish Meatballs 109

5.13 Air Fryer Fried Shrimp 110

5.14 Air Fryer Bread 111

5.15 Air Fryer Thanksgiving Turkey 111

5.16 Air Fryer Frozen Chicken Breast 112

5.17 Air Fryer Banana Bread 113

5.18 Air Fryer Veggie Chip Medley 113

5.19 Air Fryer Spareribs 114

5.20 Homemade Italian meatball air fryer 115

5.21 Twice Air Fried Vegan Stuffed Idaho Potatoes 115

5.22 Air Fryer Beef Empanadas 116

5.23 Healthy Fish Finger Sandwich & Optimum Healthy Air Fry 117

5.24 Quinoa Burgers Air fryer 117

5.25 Air Fryer Pepperoni Pizza 119

5.26 Crispy air fryer Tofu along with sticky orange sauce 120

5.27 Bourbon Bacon Burger 120

5.28 Leftover Greek Spanakopita Pie in The Air Fryer 121

5.29 Tandoori chicken 122

5.30 Air Fryer Chicken Nuggets 123

5.31 Air Fryer Ranch Chicken Tenders 124

5.32 Air fryer beef 125

5.33 Air Fryer Falafel 126

5.34 Air Fryer Bacon Burger Bites 126

5.35 Air Fryer Bacon Wrapped Scallops 127

5.36 Air Fryer Chicken Milanese With Arugula 127

5.37 Air Fryer Asian Glazed Boneless Chicken Thighs 128

5.38 Air Fryer Cajun Shrimp Dinner... 129

5.39 Easy Garlic Knots 130

5.40	Tostones (Twice air-fried plantains)	130
5.41	Stuffed Bagel Balls	131
5.42	Za'atar lamb chops	131
5.43	Air Fryer Meatballs	132
5.44	Air Fryer Salmon Patties	132
5.45	Air Fryer Salmon	133
5.46	Crispy Parmesan Crusted Chicken Breasts	134

Chapter 6: Desserts Recipes 135

6.1	Air Fryer Oreos	135
6.2	Air Fryer Roasted Bananas	135
6.3	Air Fryer Beignets	136
6.4	Air-Fried Butter Cake	136
6.5	House Gluten-Free Fresh Cherry Crumble	137
6.6	Chocolate Cake in an Air Fryer	138
6.7	Air Fryer Sweet French Toast Sticks	138
6.8	Air-Fryer Cannoli	139
6.9	Double-Glazed Air-Fried Cinnamon Biscuit Bites	140
6.10	Air Fryer Strawberry "Pop-Tarts"	141
6.11	Glazed Cake Doughnut Holes	142
6.12	Peach Hand Pies in an Air Fryer	142
6.13	Air Fryer Churros with Chocolate Sauce	143
6.14	Chocolate Orange Christmas Biscuits	144
6.15	Air fryer Oat Sandwich Biscuits	145
6.16	Half Cooked Air Fryer Lemon Biscuits	145
6.17	Melting Moments in Air fryer	146
6.18	Air Fryer Shortbread	146
6.19	Air Fryer Cupcakes	147
6.20	Air Fryer Lemon Butterfly Buns	148
6.21	Air Fryer Apple Crisp	149
6.22	Chocolate Mug Cake	149
6.23	Air Fryer Blueberry Jam Tarts	150
6.24	Chocolate Orange Chocolate Fondant	150
6.25	Air Fryer Pumpkin Pie	151
6.26	Leftover Coconut Sugar Recipes	152
6.27	Air Fryer Mince Pies	153

6.28	Air Fryer Brownies	153
6.29	Chocolate Eclairs in The Air Fryer	154
6.30	Air Fryer Chocolate Profiteroles	155
6.31	Air Fryer Doughnuts from Scratch	155
6.32	Air Fryer Baking for Easter	156
6.33	Molten lava cake	157
6.34	Basque Burnt Cheesecake	157
6.35	Banana Muffin	158

Conclusion 159

Introduction

The air fryer is basically an amped-up countertop oven. It does not actually fry the food. (Though, keep in mind that there is a difference between air-frying & baking.) Patented by Philips Electronics Corporation, the small appliance entitlements to mimic the outcomes of deep-frying with nothing more than warm air & little or no oil. This tool has surged in admiration over the last some years. Approximately 40% of U.S. houses had one as of July 2020. Obviously, the ratio will increase by 2022, according to the market survey firm NPD Group. There is every kind of thing you could air-fry—from frozen wings & homemade French fries to roasted veggies & fresh-baked cookies.

An air fryer circulates the hot air at a high velocity around the food. At the top, air begins and is then forced down by a fan. The air circulates up to the surface, and the food is cooked (like a convection oven on a smaller scale). Before placing it in the air fryer, covering the food in minimum oil tends to crunch up the food's exterior but leaves the inside soft. According to Philips, you can fry, bake, roast, or grill food in a limited period, which claims to be the "original" air fryer.

If people want to make a crunchy meal, it is time for the air fryer to heat up and start cooking. In each group, we have combined up 5-6 of our favorite meals, so you have got a baseline to start your air frying adventure. These meals will expose to the strengths of the appliance, and you will soon be able to play with a large variety of air-fried foods.

With these unforgettable air fryer meals in the air fryer, launch the day off. These Breakfast Frittata or Scotch Eggs could hit the flavor if savory is what crave early in the morning. But if the taste is sweeter, stay with the Sugar Doughnuts or Simple French Toast Sticks. Many of these meals include components that can be cooked in the afternoon unless you are in a hurry around breakfast time.

Chapter 1: What Is An Air Fryer?

1.1 Working Mechanism of Air Fryer

The top segment of an air fryer grips a heating mechanism & fan. You place the food in the fryer-style bucket & once anyone turn it on, warm air rushes down & across the food. This fast movement makes your food crunchy, similar to deep-frying but exclusive of the oil.

Here is how to use the air fryer:

1. Place the food in a basket

Depending on the air fryer's size, the basket might hold anywhere from two to ten quarts. In many cases, you will have to add one or two teaspoons of oil to make the food get good & crispy. If you are in a rush, you could put foil in the air fryer to make the cleanup a little easier.

2. Set the time & temperature

Air fryer cooking time & temperature usually range from five to twenty-five minutes at 350° to 400°F, varying on the food you are cooking.

3. Let the food cook

In a few cases, you might have to flip or maybe turn the food midway through the baking time to make it crisp up equally. Once you are done cooking, it is essential to clean the air fryer.

1.2 What could you cook in the air fryer?

Air fryers are fast, & once you realize how they work, they could be used to cook frozen foods or heat all kinds of fresh food like salmon, steak, pork chops, chicken, & veggies. Most meats need no oil because they are already so juicy: just flavor them with salt & your favorite herbs & spices. Be sure you stick to dry flavorings fewer moisture leads to crispier outcomes. If you like to sew meats with BBQ sauce or honey, stay until the last mins of cooking.

Slim cuts of red or white meat, or foods with a bit or no fat, need oil to be brown & crisp up. Coat boneless chicken breasts & pork chops with a little oil before flavoring. Canola oil or vegetable oil is typically recommended due to its high smoke point, which could stand up to the higher heat in the air fryer.

Vegetables are also required to be tossed in oil before frying. It is recommended to sprinkle them with salt before frying, but use a bit less than you are used to. The crunchy, air-fried bits packet a lot of flavors. Everyone loves broccoli florets, baby potato halves & Brussels sprouts. They come out so crunchy. Beets, Butternut squash and sweet potatoes all look to get sweeter, & green beans & peppers take little or no time at all.

1.3 How to clean the Air Fryer?

Every time you cook with the air fryer, wash your basket, tray, and pan with hot water & soap, or place them in a dishwasher. (Refer to a brand's manual to ensure these components are dishwasher reliable.) You must also swiftly clean the inside using a soggy cloth with a little dish soap on the region. Dry all the components and reunite.

4-Week Meal Plan

The meal plan is a nutrition program intended to help people achieve their weight-loss objectives through nutritious eating, portion control & daily exercise. The strategy calls for balanced consumption that includes a mixture of all the various food groups: ex carbs, com plenty of vegetables, lean protein & healthy fats. The recipes can be swapped by you in the table in order for the variation you want. Here is the recommended meal plan.

Week 1

Meal	Mon	Tue	Wed	Thu	Fri	Sat	Sun
Appetizer	Air Fryer Pickles	Air Fryer Ravioli	Air Fryer Egg Rolls	Air Fryer Pakoras	Air Fryer Arancini	Air Fryer Taco Soup	Air Fryer Crab Cake
Breakfast	Air Fryer Apple Fritters	Air Fryer Omelet	Air Fryer Crispy Bacon	Air Fryer Tofu	Air Fryer Brussel Sprouts	Air Fryer Crispy Bacon	Air Fryer Churros
Lunch	Air Fryer Potato Chips	Air Fryer Radishes	Air Fryer Steak Fajitas	Air-Fryer Pork Schnitzel	Chicken Soft Tacos	Air Fryer Eggplant Fries	Air Fryer Cumin Carrots
Dinner	Air Fryer Roast Chicken	Air Fryer Bread	Air Fryer Spareribs	Quinoa Burgers	Air Fryer Fried Shrimp	Air Fryer Banana Bread	Beef Empanadas
Dessert	Air-Fryer Cannoli	Air Fryer Brownies	Molten Lawa Cake	Cinnamon Rolls	Banana muffin	Cassava cake	Air Fryer Mince Pies

Week 2

Meal	Mon	Tue	Wed	Thu	Fri	Sat	Sun
Appetizer	Air Fryer Taquitos	Air Fryer Pepper Poppers	Spicy Pickle Fries (Dill)	Air Fryer Crab Cake	Air Fryer Pork Balls	Air Fryer Arancini	Air Fryer Coconut Shrimp
Breakfast	Air Fryer Breakfast Burritos	Air Fryer Breakfast Frittata	Air Fryer Crispy Bacon	Air Fryer Raspberry Muffins	Air Fryer Tofu	Air Fryer Brussel Sprouts	Air Fryer Churros
Lunch	Air-Fryer Papas Rellenas	Air-Fryer Shrimp Po'boys	Air-Fryer Nashville Hot Chicken	Air-Fryer Cumin Carrots	Air-Fryer Mini Chimichangas	Air-Fryer Fiesta Chicken Fingers	Air Fryer Tortellini with Prosciutto
Dinner	Air Fryer Banana Bread	Air Fryer Veggie Chip Medley	Air Fryer Pepperoni Pizza	Bourbon Bacon Burger	Air Fryer Falafel	Air fryer beef	Easy Garlic Knots
Dessert	Air Fryer Shortbread	Air Fryer Cupcakes	Basque Burnt Cheesecake	Air Fryer Mince Pies	Air Fryer Apple Crisp	Chocolate Mug Cake	Air Fryer Brownies

Week 3

Meal	Mon	Tue	Wed	Thu	Fri	Sat	Sun
Appetizer	Garlic Rosemary Sprouts	Caribban Wontons	Air Fryer Paneer Pakoras	Cheeseburger Onion Rings	Sweet & Spicy Meatballs	Air Fryer Egg Rolls	Air Fryer Cauliflower Tots
Breakfast	Air-Fryer Southern Cheese	Air Fryer Biscuit Breakfast Bombs	Air Fryer Raspb. Muffins	Air Fryer Hard Boiled Eggs	Air Fryer Crispy Bacon	Air-Fryer Southern Cheese	Air Fryer Breakfast Frittata
Lunch	Air-Fryer Papas Rellenas	Chicken Soft Tacos	Air-Fryer Ham & Egg Pockets	Air-Fryer Mini Chimichangas	Air-Fryer Quinoa Arancini	Air-Fryer Crumb-Topped Sole	Air-Fryer Fiesta Chicken Fingers
Dinner	Air fryer Reuben Calzones	Air Fryer Banana Bread	Stuffed Bagel Balls	Air Fryer Salmon Patties	Air Fryer Bacon Burger Bites	Air Fryer Thanksgiving Turkey	Bourbon Bacon Burger
Dessert	Air-Fried Butter Cake	Air Fryer Lemon Butterfly Buns	Air Fryer Baking for Easter	Air Fryer Blueberry Jam Tarts	Air Fryer Mince Pies	Banana Muffin	Melting Moments in Air fryer

Week 4

Meal	Mon	Tue	Wed	Thu	Fri	Sat	Sun
Appetizer	Air Fryer Pickles	Air Fryer Pepper Poppers	Air Fryer Egg Rolls	Air Fryer Crab Cake	Air Fryer Paneer Pakoras	Air Fryer Arancini	Cheeseburger Onion Rings
Breakfast	Air Fryer Raspberry Muffins	Air-Fryer Southern Cheese	Air Fryer Crispy Bacon	Air Fryer Hard Boiled Eggs	Air Fryer Breakfast Frittata	Air Fryer Omelet	Air Fryer Crispy Bacon
Lunch	Air-Fryer Fiesta Chicken Fingers	Air-Fryer Crumb-Topped Sole	Air-Fryer Papas Rellenas	Bang Bang Chicken	Air-Fryer Quinoa Arancini	Fish Tacos	Air-Fryer Mini Chimichangas
Dinner	Air Fryer Bacon Burger Bites	Bourbon Bacon Burger	Stuffed Bagel Balls	Air Fryer Banana Bread	Tandoori Chicken	Air Fryer Bread	Air Fryer Sparerib
Dessert	Melting Moments in Air fryer	Air Fryer Blueberry Jam Tarts	Air Fryer Baking for Easter	Air Fryer Lemon Bisquits	Molten Java Cake	Banana Muffin	Air Fryer Mug Cake

Chapter 2: Appetizer Recipes

2.1 Air Fryer Pickles

Preparation Time: 15 mins

Cooking Time: 15 mins

Servings: 12

Ingredients

- 32 pieces, dill pickle
- 1/2 cup, flour
- 1/2 tsp, salt
- 3, eggs (lightly beaten)
- 3 tsp, juice (for dill pickle)
- 1/2 tsp, garlic
- 3 cups, panko breadcrumbs
- 2 tsp, dill snipped
- Cooking mist
- Ranch sauce along with sandwiches

Steps

1. Preheat the air fryer to 400 degrees. Allow the pickles to sit on a towel for about 15 minutes, or until the liquid has nearly completely evaporated.
2. In a small bowl, combine the flour and salt. In a separate small bowl, whisk together the pickle juice, cayenne, pickle juice, & garlic powder. Combine the panko & dill in a final small dish.
3. Dip the pickles in flour mixture on both sides and shake off excess. Dip in the shell mixture, then pat in crumb mixture to help the coating adhere. In batches, arrange pickles in a single layer on an oil tray in air-fryer basket. Cook for 7-10 minutes, or until golden brown and crispy. Turn the pickles, spray with cooking oil. Cook for 7-10 minutes, or until light golden and crispy. Serve right away. If desired, top with BBQ sauce.

Nutritional Serving

80 Cal, Protein: 3 g, Carb: 16 g, Fat 1 g

2.2 Air Fryer Crispy Sriracha Spring Rolls

Preparation Time: 50 mins

Cooking Time: 10 mins

Servings: 13

Ingredients

- 2 cups, coleslaw mix
- 2 big, onions (chopped)
- 1 tbsp, soy sauce
- 1 tsp, sesame oil
- 1-pound, chicken breasts (boneless, without skin)
- 1 tsp, salt
- 8 ounces, cream cheese (2 boxes)
- 2 tbsp, sriracha chili sauce
- 24, roll wrappers
- Cooking mist
- Sweet sauce of green onions & chili additional

Steps

1. Preheat the air fryer to 360 degrees. Toss with coleslaw, green onion, sesame oil, and soy sauce & set aside while the chicken cooks. Place chicken in a thin layer on an oiled plate in an air-fryer basket. Cook for approximately 20 minutes, or until a thermometer inserted into the chicken registers 160°. Finely chop the chicken and season with salt.

2. Preheat the air fryer to 402 degrees Fahrenheit. In a large mixing bowl, combine the cream cheese & Sriracha chili sauce; stir in the chicken & coleslaw mixture. Approximately 2 tsp. 1 corner of a roll wrapper stuffed slightly below the center of the wrapper (Cover the leftover wrappers with a damp paper towel until ready to use.) Wet those remaining edges and fold its bottom corner overfilling. Overfilling, pull side corners toward the center; roll back tightly, pressing tip to close.

3. Place spring rolls in a single layer on a tray (oiled) in the air-fryer basket; spritz the cooking oil spray in batches. Cook until gently browned, about 4-5 minutes. Turn; spritz with cooking spray. Cook for another 5-6 minutes, or until crisp & golden brown. If desired, top with sweet chili sauce.

4. Option 1: Freeze an inch of raw spring rolls. Using waxed paper to separate layers in freezer containers.

Nutritional Serving

127 Cal, Protein: 6 g, Carb: 10 g, Fat 7 g

2.3 Air Fryer Fiesta Chicken Fingers

Preparation Time: 20 mins

Cooking Time: 15 mins

Servings: 4

Ingredients

- 3/4-pound, chicken breasts (boneless, without skin)

- 1/2 cup, buttermilk
- 1/4 tsp, pepper
- 1 cup, flour
- 2 cups, chips of maize (smashed)
- 1, taco seasoning envelope
- Tomato dip/sour cream ranch

Steps

1. Preheat the air fryer to 402 degrees. Using a 1/2-inch meat mallet, pound the chicken breasts. 1-inch-thick slices Strips of Long

2. In a small bowl, combine the buttermilk and pepper. In a separate shallow dish, place the flour. Combine corn chips and taco sauce in the third bowl. Dip chicken in flour to coat both sides and shake off excess. To help corn chip mixture stick to the coating, dip it in buttermilk mixture first.

3. Spray the chicken with vegetable oil and arrange it in a thin layer on an oiled pan in air-fryer basket. Cook approximately 7-8 minutes on each side, just until the chicken isn't any longer pink and the coating is gently browned. Rep with the remaining chicken. Serve with ranch dip or salsa.

Nutritional Serving

676 Cal, Protein: 24 g, Carb: 60 g, Fat 36 g

2.4 Air Fryer Cheeseburger Onion Rings

Preparation Time: 25 mins

Cooking Time: 15 mins

Servings: 8

Ingredients

- 1-pound, lean ground beef
- 1/3 cup, ketchup
- 2 tsp, mustard
- 1/2 tsp, salt
- 1, onion large
- 4 ounces, cheddar cheese
- 3/4 cup, flour
- 2 tbsp, garlic powder
- 2 big eggs (lightly beaten)
- 1 ½, panko crumbs (for bread)
- Cooking mist
- Hot ketchup

Steps

1. Preheat air fryer to 335 degrees Fahrenheit. In a large mixing basin, gently but completely combine the ketchup, salt, meat, & mustard. 1/2 onion, chopped Cut into circles; slices 8 slices of beef to cover half of beef mixture (save leftover onion rings for other use). Top each with a piece

of cheese & a different leftover meat mixture.

2. In a small bowl, combine the flour & garlic powder. Place the eggs & breadcrumbs in separate shallow dishes. Fill onion rings with flour and brush off the excess. To make this coating stick, dip it in the egg and then in the breadcrumbs.

3. Sprinkle onion rings in cooking oil spray and place in groups on oiled tray inside the air-fryer basket. Cook for 12-15 minutes, or until a meat thermometer reads 163 degrees. If desired, top with hot ketchup.

Nutritional Serving

258 Cal, Protein: 19 g, Carb: 19 g, Fat 11 g

2.5 Garlic Rosemary Sprouts

Preparation Time: 20 mins

Cooking Time: 10 mins

Servings: 4

Ingredients

- 1 tbsp, olive oil
- 2 cloves, diced garlic
- 1/2 tsp, salt
- 1/4 tsp, pepper (any)
- 1 pound, sprouts (brussels halved & trimmed)
- 1/2-pound, crumbs of panko bread
- 1 tsp, new rosemary minced

Steps

1. Preheat the air fryer to 352 degrees. Microwave the first four ingredients for 30 seconds or longer in a tiny microwave-safe dish.

2. Toss Cauliflower with a 2 teaspoon oil mixture. Put the Brussels sprouts in air-fryer basket and cook for 5-6 minutes. Sprouts should be stirred up. Cook for another eight minutes, stirring occasionally, till the sprouts are lightly browned & nearly soft.

3. Toss the breadcrumbs with the rosemary & remaining oil mixture, then top with the sprouts. Cook for another 4-5 minutes, or until crumbs are golden brown & the sprouts are tender. Serve right away.

Nutritional Serving

164 Cal, Protein: 5 g, Carb: 15 g, Fat 11 g

2.6 Air Fryer Ravioli

Preparation Time: 10 mins

Cooking Time: 10 mins

Servings: 3

Ingredients

- 1 cup, breadcrumbs

- 1/4 cup, parmesan sliced cheese
- 2 tsp, basil dried
- 1/2 cup, flour
- 2 big, lightly beaten eggs
- 9 ounces, beef ravioli (1 frozen bag)
- Cooking mist
- New basil (minced)
- Sauce of marinara, 1 cup

Steps

1. Preheat the air fryer to 350 degrees. In a small bowl, combine the parmesan cheese, basil, & breadcrumbs. Place the flour & eggs in separate shallow bowls. Now Dip ravioli into flour & shake off excess to coat all ends. Dip the shells in the crumb mixture, then pat them down to help them stick to the coating.

2. Arrange ravioli in a single layer on an oiled tray inside the air-fryer basket, and spray with cooking oil. Cook until golden brown, about 4-5 minutes. Turn; spritz with cooking spray. Cook for another 4-5 mins, or until gently browned. If required, top with basil and more Parmesan cheese right away.

Nutritional Serving

373 Cal, Protein: 17 g, Carb: 45 g, Fat 13 g

2.7 Air Fryer Taquitos

Preparation Time: 15 mins

Cooking Time: 20 mins

Servings: 6

Ingredients

- 2 big, eggs
- 1/2 cup, crumbs of dry bread
- ½ tsp, seasoning taco
- 1-pound, lean ground beef
- 6 inches, tortillas of corn (6)
- Cooking mist
- Guacamole & salsa

Steps

1. Preheat the air fryer to 352 degrees. In a large mixing bowl, combine the eggs, breadcrumbs, & taco spice. Blend in the meat well but gently.

2. 1/4 cup beef mixture should be spooned down the center of each tortilla. Coil firmly and stably using toothpicks. Spray taquitos with cooking oil spray and arrange in batches on to an tray (oiled) in the air-fryer basket. Cook for six minutes, then turn to the oven and bake until the meat is done and the taquitos are gently browned & crispy, about 7-8 minutes more. Remove the toothpicks before serving.

Nutritional Serving

174 Cal, Protein: 10 g, Carb: 12 g, Fat 9 g

2.8 Air Fryer General Tso's Cauliflower

Preparation Time: 25 mins

Cooking Time: 20 mins

Servings: 4

Ingredients

- 1/2 cup, Flour
- 1/2 cup, Cornstarch
- 1 tsp, Salt
- 1 tsp, Powder for baking
- 3/4 tsp, Soda club
- 1, cauliflower (a medium head)

Ingredients for sauce

- 1/4 cup, Fruit juice
- 3 tsp, Sugar
- 3 tbsp, Soy sauce
- 3 tsp, Vegetable broth
- 2 tbsp, Vinegar for rice
- 2 tbsp, Sesame oil
- 2 tsp, Cornstarch
- 2 tsp, Canola oil
- 3, green onions
- 3 cloves, Garlic
- 1 tsp, ginger root (freshly grated)
- 1/2 tsp, Orange zest grated
- 4 cups, Hot cooked rice

Steps

1. Preheat the air fryer to 402 degrees. Combine the salt, rice, baking powder, and cornstarch in a mixing bowl. Stir in the club soda just before serving. Toss the florets inside the batter & set them on a wire rack to cool. Allow 5 minutes for the ingredients to come together. In the air-fryer basket, put the cauliflower in batches on an oil tray. Cook for 8-12 minutes, or until soft and gently browned.

2. Meanwhile, mix together the first 6 sauce ingredients, then add the cornstarch and stir until smooth.

3. In a large saucepan, heat canola oil at medium-high heat. Cook and stir for 1-2 min, until the chiles are sour. Cook for approximately 2 minutes, till the white onions, garlic, ginger, & orange zest are tart. Add the orange juice mixture to the pot and stir well. Bring to a boil, then simmer and stir for another 2-4 minutes until it thickens.

4. Add cauliflower to the sauce and serve with rice and green onions.

Nutritional Serving

528 Cal, Protein: 11 g, Carb: 97 g, Fat 11 g

2.9 Air Fryer Nashville Hot Chicken

Preparation Time: 30 mins

Cooking Time: 10 mins

Servings: 6

Ingredients

- 2 tsp, dill pickle juice
- 2 tsp, pepper sauce (spicy)
- 1 tsp, salt
- 2 pounds, tenderloin chicken
- 1 cup, flour
- 1/2 tsp, mustard
- Egg
- 1/2 cup, buttermilk
- Cooking mist
- 1/2 cup, olive oil
- 2 tsp, cayenne pepper
- 2 cups, sugar (dark brown)
- 1 tsp, paprika
- 1 tsp, chili powder
- 1/2 tsp, garlic
- Pieces of dill pickle

Steps

1. In a cup or small dish, combine 1 tbsp pickle juice, 1 tbsp hot sauce, and 1/2 tsp salt. Refrigerate for at least 1 hour after adding the chicken. Discharge, chucking some marinade out the window.

2. Preheat an air fryer to 375°F. In a small bowl, combine the flour, the other 1/2 teaspoon salt, and the pepper. In a separate small cup, mix together all the eggs, buttermilk, 1 tbsp pickle juice, and 1 tbsp spicy sauce. Dip your chicken in flour to coat both sides and shake off the excess. Dip into the egg mix, then back into the flour mixture.

3. Spray the chicken with vegetable oil and arrange it in a single layer on the well tray in air-fryer bowl. Heat for 6-7 minutes, or until golden brown. Turn and spray with cooking spray. Cook for another 6-7 minutes, or until gently browned.

4. Splash heated chicken with a mixture of milk, brown sugar, pepper, spice, and cinnamon.

Nutritional Serving

413 Cal, Protein: 39 g, Carb: 21 g, Fat 20 g

2.10 Air Fryer Pumpkin Fries

Preparation Time: 25 mins

Cooking Time: 15 mins

Servings: 4

Ingredients

- 1/2 cup, Greek yogurt (plain)
- 2 cups, maple syrup
- 3 tsp, chipotle peppers (minced)
- 1/8 tsp, sodium
- 1, pumpkin
- 1/4 tsp, garlic
- 1/4 tsp, ground cumin
- 1/4 tsp, chili powder
- 1/4 tsp, pepper

Steps

1. In a shallow cup, combine the chipotle peppers, maple syrup, yogurt, & 1/6 teaspoon salt. Refrigerate until ready to serve.
2. Preheat an air fryer to 402°F. Peel the pumpkin and cut it in half lengthwise. To toast the seeds, discard them. Cut into 1/4-inch wide strips. Transfer to a large mixing bowl. 1/4 teaspoon leftover pepper, cumin, garlic powder, salt, & chili powder are sprinkled over top.
3. In an air-fryer basket, arrange pumpkins in sections on an oiled surface. Cook for 8 minutes or until soft. Cook till light golden and crisp.

Nutritional Serving

151 Cal, Protein: 5 g, Carb: 31 g, Fat 3 g

2.11 Sweet & Spicy Air Fryer Meatballs

Preparation Time: 30 mins

Cooking Time: 15 mins

Servings: 6

Ingredients

- 2/3 cup, oats (for quick-cooking)
- 1/2 cup, ritz crackers
- 2, eggs (beaten)
- 5 ounces, milk
- 1 tbsp, onion (minced)
- 1 tsp, salt
- 1 tsp, garlic
- 1 tsp, cumin ground
- 1 tsp, honey
- 1/2 tsp, mustard
- 2 pounds, beef

For sauce

- 1/3 cup, Brown sugar
- 1/3 cup, Honey ()
- 1/3 cup, Orange marmalade ()
- 2 tsp, Cornstarch (.)

- 2 tsp, Soy sauce (.)
- 1-2 tsp, hot sauce (Louisiana-style)
- 1 tbsp, Worcestershire sauce

Steps

1. Preheat the air fryer to 380 degrees. In a large mixing basin, combine the first 10 ingredients. Blend in the meat well but gently. Form 1-1/4-inch balls.

2. Arrange the meatballs in a single layer on an oil tray inside an air-fryer basket. Cook approximately 14-15 minutes, or until completely cooked & golden. Meanwhile, in a small pot, add the sauce ingredients. Over medium heat, cook & stir until it thickens.

Nutritional Serving

90 Cal, Protein: 6 g, Carb: 10 g, Fat 3 g

2.12 Air Fryer Ham & Cheese Turnovers

Preparation Time: 20 mins

Cooking Time: 10 mins

Servings: 4

Ingredients

- 13.8 ounces, pizza crust (refrigerated)
- 1/4-pound, black forest deli ham
- 1, pear (medium)
- 1/4 cup, walnuts (sliced & toasted)
- 2 tsp, blue cheese crumbled

Steps

1. Preheat the air fryer to 400 degrees. On a lightly floured board, roll the pizza dough into a 14-inch piece. Cut into four triangles. Over half of the each square, diagonally layer ham, half pear slices, walnuts, and blue cheese to within 1/4 inch of the edges. Fold one corner to the other corner to form a triangle over filling; use a fork to seal the edges.

2. Place the turnovers in a single layer on an oiled tray inside the air-fryer basket and spray with such a cooking mist. Cook for 5-6 minutes, or until gently browned. Finish with the remaining pear slices.

Nutritional Serving

357 Cal, Protein: 15 g, Carb: 55 g, Fat 10 g

2.13 Air Fryer Pepper Poppers

Preparation Time: 20 mins

Cooking Time: 10 mins

Servings: 6

Ingredients

- 8 ounces, cream cheese (1 bag)
- 3/4 cup, cheddar cheese
- 3/4 cup, Monterey jack cheese (sliced)
- 6, bacon strips (fried & crumbled)

- 1/4 tsp, salt
- 1/4 tsp, garlic
- 1/4 tsp, chili powder
- 1/4 tsp, paprika
- 1-pound, fresh jalapenos
- 1/2 cup, breadcrumbs

Optional:

- Sour cream
- French onion dip
- Seasoning for ranch salad

Steps

1. Preheat the air fryer to 325 degrees. Mix the bacon, cheeses, and seasonings in a large mixing bowl. Fill each side of the pepper with roughly 1 tablespoon of breadcrumbs.
2. Operate in batches if required and arrange poppers inside a single layer in basket. Cook for 14 mins for a spicy flavor, 22 minutes for medium, and 26 minutes for moderate. If desired, top with crème fraiche or sauce.

Nutritional Serving

160 Cal, Protein: 4 g, Carb: 3 g, Fat 13 g

2.14 Air Fryer Wasabi Crab Cakes

Preparation Time: 20 mins

Cooking Time: 10 mins

Servings: 10

Ingredients

- 1 medium, red pepper
- 1, celery rib
- 3, green onions
- 2 big, egg whites
- 3 tsp, mayonnaise
- 1/4 tsp, wasabi
- 1/4 tsp, salt
- 1/3 cup, breadcrumbs
- 1-1 ½ cup, lump crabmeat
- Cooking mist

for sauce

- 1 celery (diced)
- 1/3 cup, mayonnaise
- 1, green onion
- 1 tbsp, pickle
- 1/2 tsp, wasabi
- 1/4 tsp, salt

Steps

1. Preheat the air fryer to 370 degrees. First, combine 7 components, replacing 1/4 cup of breadcrumbs. Gently fold in the crab.

2. Place the remaining breadcrumbs in a small bowl. Place crumbs in piles of crab mixture teaspoons. Softly form and cover 3/4-inch-thick patties. Place steamed crabs in a thin layer on to an oil air-fryer pan in batches. Spray crab cakes with cooking spray before frying them. Heat for 12 minutes, or until lightly browned, carefully flipping midway through cooking & sprinkling with more cooking oil spray.

3. Meanwhile, combine sauce ingredients in a food processor and pulse 3-4 times so mix or to desired consistency. Serve the crab cakes immediately with the dipping sauce.

Nutritional Serving

49 Cal, Protein: 3 g, Carb: 4 g, Fat 2 g

2.15 Air Fryer Caribbean Wontons

Preparation Time: 30 mins

Cooking Time: 10 mins

Servings: 12

Ingredients

- 4 ounces, cream cheese
- 1/4 cup, coconut (shredded)
- 1/4 cup, banana mashed
- 2 tsp, diced walnuts
- 2 tbsp, pineapple (crushed canned)
- 1 cup, marshmallow cream
- 24, wonton wrappers
- Cooking mist

for sauce

- 1 pound, strawberries ()
- 1/4 cup, sugar ()
- 1 tsp, cornstarch (.)
- Ground & sugar-cinnamon of confectioners

Steps

1. Preheat the air fryer to 350 degrees. In a small mixing bowl, beat the cream cheese until smooth. Combine the mango, banana, pineapple, & walnuts in a mixing bowl.

2. Put a wonton wrapper in your direction with 1 point. Cover the leftover wrappers with a moist paper towel until ready to use. Place 2 teaspoons of filling in the center of the wrapper. Wet the sides, then fold opposite corners so overfilling &

press together to seal. Rep with the remaining filling and wrappers.

3. Spray a greased tray inside the air-fryer basket with cooking spray and arrange wontons in a single layer. Cook for 8-12 mins, or till crisp and gently browned.

4. Meanwhile, place strawberries inside a food processor, cover, and purée until smooth. In a small saucepan, combine the sugar & cornstarch. Add the strawberry purée and mix well. Bring to a boil, then simmer for 3 minutes, stirring constantly, until the sauce thickens. If preferred, remove the combination, save the sauce, and discard the seeds. Confectioners' sugar and cinnamon are sprinkled over the wontons.

Nutritional Serving

83 Cal, Protein: 1 g, Carb: 13 g, Fat 3 g

2.16 Air fryer Beefy Swiss Bundles

Preparation Time: 20 mins

Cooking Time: 15 mins

Servings: 5

Ingredients

- 1 pound, beef
- 1 – 1 ½, mushrooms
- 1- 1 ½ tsp, onion (sliced)
- 1- 1 ½ tsp, garlic
- 2 cups, sauce Worcestershire
- 3/4 tsp, dry rosemary
- 3/4 tsp, paprika
- 1/2 tsp, salt
- 1/4 tsp, pepper
- 1, puff pastry (frozen)
- 2/3 cup, potatoes (mashed)
- 1 cup, Swiss cheese (shredded)
- 1, egg
- 2 tbsp, water

Steps

1. Preheat air fryer to 380 degrees Fahrenheit. Cook your beef, mushrooms, & onion in a large pan over medium heat for 10-12 minutes, or till the meat isn't any longer pink & the veggies are soft. Stir in the garlic and cook for another minute. Combine the sauce and Worcestershire spices in a mixing bowl.

2. On a lightly floured surface, roll pastry into a 16x13-inch square. With rectangles, cut into four 7-1/2x6-1/2-in sections. Spread 2 tsp potatoes over each rectangle, spreading to within 1 inch of the edges. 3/4 cup meat mixture on top of each; 1/4 cup cheese on top.

3. Brush some of the egg & water over the pastry's edges. Place opposing pastry

edges over each bundle and squeeze the seams together to seal them. Rub together the shells that are left behind. Place the pastry in batches on the tray inside the air-fryer basket and cook for 10-12 minutes, or until golden brown.

4. Unbaked pastries may be stored on a baking sheet (parchment-lined) until they are solid. Return to freezer in a watertight bag. Cook frozen pastries till light brown, then cook for a further 20-25 minutes.

Nutritional Serving

706 Cal, Protein: 35 g, Carb: 44 g, Fat 42 g

2.17 Air Fryer Tortellini with Prosciutto

Preparation Time: 25 mins

Cooking Time: 10 mins

Servings: 12

Ingredients

- 1 tbsp, olive oil
- 3 tbsp, onion (finely chopped)
- 4 cloves, garlic
- 15 ounces, puree tomato (1 can)
- 1 tbsp, fresh basil (minced)
- 1/4 tsp, salt
- 1/4 tsp, pepper

for tortellini

- 2, eggs
- 2 tbsp, milk
- 2/3 cup, breadcrumbs
- 1 tsp, garlic
- 2 tsp, pecorino Romano cheese (grated)
- 1 tbsp, parsley (minced & fresh)
- 1/2 tsp, salt
- 1 package, prosciutto tortellini ricotta
- Cooking mist

Steps

1. In a small saucepan, heat the oil over medium-high heat. Cook & stir for 4-5 mins, till the onion & garlic are tender. Mix in the tomato puree, basil, salt, and pepper. Bring to a boil and cook for around ten minutes.

2. Also, prepare the fryer to 350 degrees. In a small cup, whisk together the eggs and milk. In a separate dish, combine the garlic powder, salt, cheese, parsley, & breadcrumbs.

3. Toss the tortellini in the egg mixture before coating it in bread crumbs. Sprinkle tortellini with cooking spray and arrange in batches in the fryer basket on a prepared tray. Cook until golden brown, about 5-6 minutes. Turn and spray with

cooking spray. Cook for 5-6 minutes, or until gently browned.

Nutritional Serving

38 Cal, Protein: 1 g, Carb: 5 g, Fat 1 g

2.18 Air Fryer Crispy Curry Drumsticks

Preparation Time: 35 mins

Cooking Time: 15 mins

Servings: 4

Ingredients

- 1 pound, drumsticks of chicken
- 3/4 tsp, salt
- 2 tbsp, olive oil
- 2 tsp, curry powder
- 1/2 tsp, onion salt
- 1/2 tsp, garlic
- Coriander (minced)

Steps

1. Cover the chicken with water in the large mixing basin. Allow for 20 minutes at room temperature after adding 1/2 teaspoon salt.
2. Preheat an air fryer to 380°F. In a separate dish, combine the garlic powder, oil, curry powder, onion salt, and the remaining 1/4 teaspoon salt; add the chicken and toss to coat. Put the chicken in batches on the air-fryer tray in a single layer. Cook for 17-18 minutes, turning halfway through, or until a chicken, thermometer registers 175-180°. If desired, garnish with cilantro.

Nutritional Serving

180 Cal, Protein: 15 g, Carb: 1 g, Fat 13 g

2.19 Air Fryer Rosemary Sausage Meatballs

Preparation Time: 10 mins

Cooking Time: 5 mins

Servings: 2

Ingredients

- 2 tbsp, olive oil
- 4 cloves, garlic
- 1 tsp, curry (powdered)
- 1, egg
- 4 ounces, diced peppers (1 jar)
- 1/4 cup, breadcrumbs
- 1/4 cup, parsley (fresh & minced)
- 1 tbsp, rosemary (minced)
- 2 kilos, pork sausage

Steps

1. Preheat the air fryer to 450 degrees. In a medium baking dish, heat oil over

medium heat and stir-fry the curry powder & garlic until soft, about 2-3 minutes.

2. In a dish, whisk together the pepper, breadcrumbs, eggs, rosemary, parsley, & garlic combination. Sausage should be completely mixed but gently.

3. To form the 1-1/3 in. Construct the little balls. Place in a single layer on tray in the air fryer basket; cook for 8-10 minutes, or till golden brown & cooked through. If preferred, serve with pretzels.

Nutritional Serving

96 Cal, Protein: 4 g, Carb: 2 g, Fat 8 g

2.20 Air Fryer Egg Rolls

Preparation Time: 35 mins

Cooking Time: 15 mins

Servings: 10

Ingredients

- 2 cups, boiling water
- 3 cups sprouts (for beans)
- 1 pound, chicken
- 6, green onions (sliced)
- 1 tbsp, ginger root (minced)
- 3 cloves, garlic
- 1 container, sauce of Chinese-style
- 1 tbsp, soy sauce
- 1 tsp, soya sauce
- 14 ounces, coleslaw mix (1 bag)
- 10 ounces, chopped frozen spinach (1 bag)
- 18, egg roll or wrappers

Steps

1. In a small dish, pour warm water so over bean sprouts and let aside for 5 minutes. Aside from that, roast the chicken in a moderately hot oven until it is no longer pink, around 6-10 minutes. Garlic, green onions, & ginger should be added now. Cook for 2 minutes before rinsing. Switch to a large basin and stir in ½ cup fish sauce & soy sauce in a Chinese manner. Clean the frying pan.

2. In the same skillet, cook and toss the spinach, coleslaw, & drained bean sprouts until crisp-tender, about 5-6 minutes.

3. Preheat the air fryer to 400°F. With one egg roll wrapper corner, place 1/4 cup filling right below the wrapper's center. (Cover the leftover wrappers with a moist paper towel until ready to use.) Moisten the surplus wrapping edges with water and fold the bottom corner over the contents. Fold the side corners into the center of the filling. Roll the egg tightly and press down on tip to seal it.

4. Coat (greased) air-fryer basket with cooking spray and arrange the egg rolls in stages in the single layer. Cook until gently

browned, 12-14 minutes. For extra cooking, turn and spray with cooking spray. 5-6 minutes more to cook till golden brown. With the remaining sauce, serve.

Nutritional Serving

135 Cal, Protein: 7 g, Carb: 9 g, Fat 8 g

2.21 Air Fryer Turkey Croquettes

Preparation Time: 35 mins

Cooking Time: 15 mins

Servings: 5

Ingredients

- 2 cups, potatoes (mashed)
- 1/2 cup, parmesan grated cheese
- 1/2 cup, Swiss cheese (shredded)
- 1, shallot (thinly sliced)
- 2 tsp, rosemary (fresh & minced)
- 1 tsp, sage (fresh minced)
- 1/2 tsp, salt
- 1/4 tsp, pepper
- 3 cups, turkey (cooked)
- 1, egg
- 2 tsp, water
- 1/4 cup, breadcrumbs
- Frying mist along with butter fragrance

Steps

1. Preheat air fryer to 355 degrees Fahrenheit. In a large mixing bowl, combine the shallot, mashed potatoes, rosemary, cheese, salt, pepper, & sage; stir in the turkey. Create 1-inch-thick patties.

2. In a small bowl, whisk together the egg and water. Place the breadcrumbs in a third deep cup. To make coating stick, dip the croquettes inside the egg mixture and then pat them into the breadcrumbs.

3. Place the croquettes in one layer on a prepared tray in the air-fryer basket; spritz with cooking oil. Cook for 5-6 minutes, or until gold brown. Turn and spray with cooking spray. Heat until gold brown, about 5-6 minutes. If desired, top with sour cream.

Nutritional Serving

141 Cal, Protein: 5 g, Carb: 13 g, Fat 7 g

2.22 Air Fryer Cauliflower Tots

Preparation Time: 5 mins

Cooking Time: 10 mins

Servings: 4

Ingredients

- 1, nonstick spray
- 16 ounces, cauliflower tots (1 box)

Steps

1. Preheat the air fryer to 450 degrees Fahrenheit. Spray air fryer basket with nonstick cooking spray.
2. Place as many cauliflower tots as you can in the basket, making sure they don't touch.
3. In a preheated air fryer, cook for 8 minutes. Remove the basket, flip the tots, and cook for another 3 minutes, or till golden brown & done.

Nutritional Serving

147 Cal, Protein: 2 g, Carb: 20 g, Fat 6 g

2.23 Spicy Pickle Fries (Dill)

Preparation Time: 15 mins

Cooking Time: 15 mins

Servings: 12

Ingredients

- 16 ounces, dill pickle jar (spicy)
- 1 cup, flour
- 1 cup, breadcrumbs
- 1/4 cup, milk
- 1/2 tsp, paprika
- Cooking mist
- 1, egg

Steps

1. Pickles should be washed and patted dry.
2. In a mixing basin, combine flour and paprika. In a separate dish, whisk together the milk and the beaten egg. In a third bowl, add the panko.
3. Preheat an air fryer to 410°F.
4. Place a pickle on a tray and coat it with flour, egg, and breadcrumbs until it is completely coated. Rep with the remaining pickles. Spray the pickles lightly with cooking spray.
5. Place pickles in the single layer in air fryer basket; if necessary, cook in groups to avoid overflowing the fryer. Set a timer for 16 minutes and swap the pickles halfway through.

Nutritional Serving

80 Cal, Protein: 3 g, Carb: 16 g, Fat 1 g

2.24 Stuffed Mushroom with Sour Cream

Preparation Time: 35 mins

Cooking Time: 15 mins

Servings: 24

Ingredients

- 24, mushrooms (medium)
- ½, Bell pepper (green & diced)

- ½, Onion (sliced)
- 1 thin, carrot (diced)
- 2, bacon strips (sliced)
- 1 cup, Cheddar cheese (shredded)
- ½ cup, sour cream
- 1 ½ tsp, Cheddar cheese (sliced)

Steps

1. In a pan over medium heat, combine the bacon, mushroom, stems, cabbage, orange bell pepper, & carrot. 5 minutes of stirring and cooking 1 cup sour cream & cheddar cheese, stirred in; heat for two minutes, or until the filling is completely combined and the cheese has melted.
2. Preheat the oven to 180 degrees Fahrenheit.
3. Put the mushroom caps on the baking pan. Add filling to every mushroom cap in a grating pattern. 1 1/2 tablespoons Cheddar cheese, grated
4. In the air fryer's basket, place the mushroom tray. Cook for about eight minutes, or until the cheese melts.

Nutritional Serving

41 Cal, Protein: 2.1 g, Carb: 1.7 g, Fat 3 g

2.25 Honey Sriracha Air Fryer Wings

Preparation Time: 10 mins

Cooking Time: 25 mins

Servings: 2

Ingredients

- 12 each, chicken wing drumettes
- 1/2 tsp, salt
- 1/2 tbsp, garlic (powdered)
- 1 tbsp, butter
- 1/4 cup, honey
- 2 tsp, vinegar
- 1 tbsp, sriracha sauce

Steps

1. With an air fryer, preheat to 365 degree F.
2. In a cup, combine the chicken wings, garlic powder, and salt, and toss to coat.
3. Put the wings in air fryer basket. Cook the wings for 27 minutes while shaking basket every 8-9 mins. When the timer goes off, turn off the air fryer and leave the wings in the basket for another 5 mins.
4. Meanwhile, melt butter in a small saucepan over medium heat. Bring the butter, sugar, vinegar, rice, & sriracha sauce to a simmer in a saucepan. Turn the heat off.

5. Combine the fried wings & sauce in a mixing basin.

Nutritional Serving

586 Cal, Protein: 37 g, Carb: 36 g, Fat 32 g

2.26 Air Fryer Buffalo Ranch Chickpeas

Preparation Time: 5 mins

Cooking Time: 20 mins

Servings: 2

Ingredients

- 15 ounces, chickpeas
- 2 tbsp, buffalo wing sauce
- 1 tbsp, ranch dressing

Steps

1. With an air fryer, heat to 325 degrees F.
2. Prepare a baking sheet with paper towels. Chickpeas should be spread on paper towels. Place a piece of paper towel over the chickpeas and gently press to absorb any excess liquid.
3. In a saucepan, place the chickpeas. Toss in the wing sauce to combine. Salad dressing should be mixed and applied. Put the chickpeas inside an air fryer basket in an equal layer.
4. Cook it for 8 mins. Shake & cook for a further five minutes. Cook after another five minutes of shaking. Shake and heat for the last two minutes. Allow five minutes for cooling before serving.

Nutritional Serving

177 Cal, Protein: 77 g, Carb: 33 g, Fat 1.8 g

2.27 Air Fryer Sweet Potato Tots

Preparation Time: 10 mins

Cooking Time: 5 mins

Servings: 4

Ingredients

- 2, potatoes (sweet)
- ½ tsp, Seasoning Cajun
- Cooking mist along with olive oil
- Sea salt to favor

Steps

1. Add some potatoes to a saucepan of boiling water. Cook until the potatoes can be pierced with a fork but are still firm, about 20 mins. Allow for cooling after soaking.
2. Potatoes are ground into a dish using a box grater. Carefully incorporate the Cajun spice. To make the tots, mold the mixture into cylinders.
3. Spray olive oil into the air fryer basket. Place the tots in the basket in a single row, without touching the container's sides or

each other. Sprinkle the tots with sea salt after spraying them with olive oil.

4. Preheat the air fryer at 400 degrees F & cook tots for 8 mins. Switch, spritz with olive oil, and sprinkle with salt. Cook for a further 8 mins.

Nutritional Serving

311 Cal, Protein: 2.8 g, Carb: 11 g, Fat 20 g

2.28 Air Fryer Korean Chicken Wings

Preparation Time: 25 mins

Cooking Time: 10 mins

Servings: 4

Ingredients

- 1/4 cup, hot honey
- 3 tsp, gochujang
- 1 tbsp, brown sugar
- 1 tbsp, soy sauce
- 1 tsp, lemon juice
- 2 tsp, garlic (minced)
- 1 tsp, fresh ginger
- 1/2 tsp, salt
- 1/4 tsp, black pepper
- 1/4 tsp. Green onions (finely chopped)
- Ingredients for wings

- 2 kg, chicken wings
- 1 tsp, salt
- 1 tsp, garlic
- 1 tsp, onion powder
- 1 tsp, black pepper
- 1/2 cup, cornstarch

for garnishes

- 2 scoops green onions (Sliced)
- 1 tsp, Sesame seed

Steps

1. Mix the gochujang, brown sugar, soy sauce, hot honey, lime juice, salt, garlic, ginger, & black pepper together in a pot. Bring the sauce to the boil over medium heat, then lower to a low heat and let it simmer for 6 mins. Stir in green onions before serving.

2. Preheat the air fryer to 450 degrees Fahrenheit.

3. Place the wings in a large mixing bowl and season with salt, garlic powder, onion powder, & black pepper. Toss the wings in cornstarch until they're completely coated. Shake each wing before placing it in the steamer basket to make sure that it does not contact the others; if necessary, cook in batches.

4. In a hot air fryer, cook for 15 minutes, then shake the basket & cook for another 12

minutes. Flip the wings and cook for another 7-10 minutes, or till the chicken is done.

5. Soak each wing inside the sauces & then add the sesame seeds & chopped green onions to the marinade. Serve with the remaining sauce on the side.

Nutritional Serving

97 Cal, Protein: 13.5 g, Carb: 0 g, Fat 7 g

2.29 Air Fried Mozzarella Sticks

Preparation Time: 15 mins

Cooking Time: 10 mins

Servings: 3

Ingredients

for batter

- 1/2 cup, water
- 1/4 cup, flour
- 5 tsp, cornstarch
- 1 tbsp, cornmeal
- 1 tsp, garlic
- 1/2 tsp, salt

for coatings

- 1 cup, breadcrumbs
- 1/2 tsp, salt
- 1/2 tsp, black pepper
- 1/2 tsp, flakes of parsley
- 1/2 tsp, garlic (powdered)
- 1/4 tsp, onion
- 1/4 tsp, dried oregano
- 1/4 tsp, dry basil
- 5 ounces, mozzarella cheese
- 1 tbsp, flour
- Cooking mist

Steps

1. Combine cornstarch, water, cornmeal, garlic powder, flour, & salt in a large, shallow cup; whisk to combine the pancake batter's consistency. Change the components as required to get the desired quality.

2. Combine the parsley, panko, pepper, salt, onion powder, oregano, garlic powder, and basil in a large shallow cup.

3. Thinly coat each mozzarella stick with flour. Dip each stick in the batter then in panko mixture. Arrange the sticks inside a single layer on a baking sheet. Freeze for at least one hour.

4. As directed by the manufacturer, preheat an air fryer to 450 º F. In the fryer basket, arrange a series of mozzarella sticks. For frying, apply a little coating of spray. On sticks, cook for six minutes. Open the fryer & turn the sticks with a spatula. Cook for

another 9-10 minutes, or until gently browned.

Nutritional Serving

69 Cal, Protein: 2.8 g, Carb: 18 g, Fat 0 g

2.30 Air Fryer Pakoras

Preparation Time: 15 mins

Cooking Time: 10 mins

Servings: 3

Ingredients

- 2 cups, cauliflower (sliced)
- 1 cup, potatoes (diced)
- 1 ¼ cups, chickpea flour
- 3/4 cup, water
- 1/2 tbsp, red onion (chopped)
- 1 tbsp, salt
- 1 clove, garlic
- 1 tsp, curry (powdered)
- 1 tsp, cilantro
- 1/2 tsp, cayenne pepper
- 1/2 tsp, cumin
- Cooking spray

Steps

1. Combine the water, curry powder, salt, potatoes, red onion, pepper, cayenne cilantro, chickpea flour, cauliflower, garlic, & cumin in a large mixing basin. Set aside 10 minutes to unwind.
2. Preheat the air fryer to 180°C.
3. Spray the cooking spray on the air-fryer basket. Fill the basket halfway with the cauliflower mixture & smooth it out. Rep, avoiding touching the pakoras.
4. Cook for another 8 minutes after flipping. Place it on a dish covered with paper towels. Rep with the remaining batter.

Nutritional Serving

50 Cal, Protein: 17 g, Carb: 3 g, Fat 15 g

2.31 Bacon Wrapped Scallops along with Sriracha Mayo

Preparation Time: 15 mins

Cooking Time: 20 mins

Servings: 9

Ingredients

- 1/2 cup, mayonnaise
- 2 tbsp, sriracha sauce
- 1 pound, bay scallops
- 1 pinch, salt
- 1 pinch, black pepper
- 12 strips, bacon
- Cooking mist along with olive oil

Steps

1. Combine the Sriracha sauce & mayonnaise in a small bowl. Refrigerate the Sriracha mayo until ready to use.
2. Preheat the air fryer to 395 degrees F.
3. Spread the scallops out on a tray and rinse them with a paper towel. Season with pepper and salt. Seal each scallop with a quarter slice of bacon.
4. Spray an air fryer basket with vegetable oil. Place bacon-wrapped scallops inside a single layer inside the basket; break into two rounds if required.
5. Cook for 7 minutes in an air fryer. Check for doneness; scallops should be transparent, and bacon should be crunchy. Cook 1 to 2 minutes longer if necessary, testing every minute. With tongs, carefully select the scallops and drain the bacon fat. Serve with Sriracha mayonnaise.

Nutritional Serving

222 Cal, Protein: 17 g, Carb: 3 g, Fat 15 g

2.32 Air Fryer Balsamic Glazed Chicken Wings

Preparation Time: 10 mins

Cooking Time: 25 mins

Servings: 2

Ingredients

for coatings

- Cooking mist
- 3 tbsp, baking powder
- 2 tbsp, salt
- 1 tbsp, black pepper (freshly ground)
- 1 tsp, paprika
- 2 pounds, chicken legs

for glaze

- 1/3 cup, water
- 1/3 cup, balsamic vinegar
- 2 tsp, soy sauce
- 2 tsp, honey
- 2 tsp, chili sauce
- 2 cloves, garlic (minced)
- 1 tsp, water
- 1 tsp, cornstarch

for Garnish

- 1, onion
- 1/4 tsp, sesame seeds

Steps

1. With an air fryer, heat to 385 ° F. Cooking oil should be poured into the fryer basket.
2. Combine the cinnamon, baking powder, pepper, & paprika in a small cup. Place a few of chicken wings in a bag with a

baking powder mixture and shake to coat. Remove the wings from of the jar, brush off the leftover flour, & continue till all the wings are coated in the baking powder mixture.

3. Brush the wings with cooking oil, place them in the steamer basket, & cook for 20 mins, shaking & turning halfway through. Increase the temp up to 450 °F & bake for another 5 minutes or until crispy. Depending on the size of your air fryer, you'll have to prepare the wings in batches.

4. Meanwhile, combine balsamic vinegar, honey, 1/4 cup water, chili sauce, soy sauce, and garlic in a skillet over medium heat. Bring to a low boil & cook for about fifteen minutes, or till the sauce has reduced. Combine 1 tsp water and cornstarch in a shallow cup and stir into the sauce until it thickens.

5. Place the crispy wings in a wide cup, add the sauce, & swirl till thoroughly covered.

Nutritional Serving

458 Cal, Protein: 32 g, Carb: 32 g, Fat 22 g

2.33 Air Fryer Loaded Greek Fries

Preparation Time: 10 mins

Cooking Time: 30 mins

Servings: 4

Ingredients

- 1/2 small, cucumber
- 1/2 tsp, salt
- 6 ounces, Greek yogurt
- 1 tbsp, lemon juice
- 2 tsp, dill (freeze-dried)
- 1 tsp, garlic (minced)
- 1 tsp, vinegar
- 4 ounces, cheese box (crumbled feta)
- 4, russet potatoes (medium-sized)
- 2 tsp, olive oil
- 2 tsp, Greek seasoning
- Cooking mist
- 1 small, red onion (sliced into strips)
- 1/4 cup, kalamata olives (sliced)
- 12, grape tomatoes (each halved)

Steps

1. In a sieve, shred the cucumber and season it with salt. Allow it to drain for 10 minutes.

2. In a small bowl, combine the dill, vinegar, milk, garlic, lemon juice, and feta to make the remainder of the tzatziki. Once everything is evenly blended, stir it again. When ready to use, stir in shredded cucumber and set aside.

3. With an air fryer, heat to 450 degrees F.

4. Combine the fries, olive oil, & Greek spices in a large mixing bowl & toss until well combined. Coat the pan of the air fryer with nonstick cooking spray. 1/2 of fries should be added to the basket.

5. In an air fryer, cook for 10 minutes. When done, flip and bake for another 5 minutes or so for the ideal crispness. Repeat with the remaining fries.

6. Divide the fries among four plates to serve. Drizzle cucumber sauce so over top of a fries. On each plate, marinate the olives, Kalamata olives, red onion strips, & grape tomatoes.

Nutritional Serving

350 Cal, Protein: 11 g, Carb: 47 g, Fat 13 g

2.34 Air Fryer Arancini

Preparation Time: 20 mins

Cooking Time: 20 mins

Servings: 5

Ingredients

- 3 big, chickens
- 1/2 cups, rice (cooked)
- 2/3 cup, parmesan cheese (grated)
- 1/3 cup, sugar (melted)
- 1/2 tsp, Italian cheese
- 1/2 tsp, salt
- 1/4 tsp, black pepper
- 2 ounces, mozzarella cheese
- 1 cup, breadcrumbs
- 1/2 tsp, Italian seasoning
- 1 pinch, salt
- 1 pinch, black pepper
- Cooking mist nonstick

Steps

1. 2 eggs, lightly beaten inside a wide cup Blend in the parmesan cheese, sugar, flour, garlic, 1/4 teaspoon salt, and 1/2 teaspoon pepper until well combined. With the combination, cover & refrigerate for 22 minutes.

2. Preheat the oven to 375 degrees Fahrenheit.

3. Make a 1 1/2-inch circle out of the mixture. Reshape each ball by pressing a piece of mozzarella into to the center.

4. Combine the pepper, panko breadcrumbs, salt, & Italian seasoning in a small bowl. Gently whisk the remaining egg in a separate dish. Each rice ball should be dipped in the eggs first, then rolled in the panko mixture. Spray the rice balls with cooking spray and place them in the air fryer basket.

5. In a preheated air fryer, cook for 6 minutes. Increase the heat to 450 ° F & continue to cook the air for 3 mins.

Nutritional Serving

385 Cal, Protein: 15 g, Carb: 21 g, Fat 38 g

2.35 Air Fryer Mac & Cheese Ball

Preparation Time: 20 mins

Cooking Time: 60 mins

Servings: 24

Ingredients

- 6 cups, water
- 7.12-ounce, macaroni & cheese (1 bag)
- 1/4 cup, milk
- 4 tbsp, margarine
- 3/4 cup, cheddar cheese (shredded & sharp)
- Cooking mist (nonstick)
- 1/2 cup, panko breadcrumbs
- 1/2 cup, breadcrumbs
- 1/2 tsp, salt
- 1/2 tbsp, garlic (powdered)
- 2, eggs

Steps

1. Fill a dish halfway with water and bring to a boil. In a large mixing bowl, combine the spaghetti macaroni from the supper box. Cook, stirring occasionally, for 6 to 8 minutes, or until soft. Please drain rather than wash. Return the saucepan to the stove and whisk inside the cheese sauce, including the milk and margarine. Attach cheddar cheese & stir until it has melted and is evenly distributed.

2. Refrigerate macaroni and cheese until solid, anything from 2 hrs. to midnight.

3. Make 1/2-inch balls out of the macaroni & cheese and place them on a cooking sheet lined along with parchment paper.

4. Preheat a fryer to 355°F. Use nonstick cooking spray to coat the basket.

5. Combine the panko, breadcrumbs, salt, & garlic powder in a medium mixing bowl. Dip every ball into the beaten eggs, then into the panko mixture.

6. Place the mac & cheese balls inside the air fryer basket in a single layer, making sure they don't touch, and cook in batches if necessary.

7. Cook for 8 to 12 minutes in a preheated air fryer. Switch to the other side of the pan and cook for another three or four minutes, or until gently browned.

Nutritional Serving

87 Cal, Protein: 3 g, Carb: 9 g, Fat 4 g

2.36 Air Fryer Fingerling Potatoes with Dip

Preparation Time: 10 mins

Cooking Time: 15 mins

Servings: 2

Ingredients

- 12 ounces, fingerling potatoes
- 1 tbsp, olive oil
- 1 tsp, garlic
- 1/4 tsp, paprika
- Salt n pepper (ground black)

Sauce:

- 1/3 cup, sour cream
- 2 ounces, mayonnaise
- 2 tsp, parmesan cheese (finely grated)
- 1 ½ tsp, ranch dressing
- 1 spoon, white vinegar
- 1 tbsp, new parsley (chopped)

Steps

1. Preheat an air fryer to 395 degrees F for five minutes.
2. Place potatoes in a dish with paprika, olive oil, pepper, garlic powder, and salt. Toss until the potatoes are completely coated, then transfer to the air fryer basket.
3. Cook for 18 to 30 minutes in a hot air fryer, shaking midway through the basket until the potatoes are cooked through and crispy.
4. While the potatoes are cooking, combine the sour cream, mayonnaise, ranch dressing mix, parmesan cheese, & vinegar in a small basin.
5. Place the fried potatoes on a platter and top with parsley. Serve immediately with dipping sauce.

Nutritional Serving

385 Cal, Protein: 7 g, Carb: 36 g, Fat 24 g

2.37 Air Fryer Taco Soup

Preparation Time: 10 mins

Cooking Time: 13 mins

Servings: 6

Ingredients

- 4 inches, corn tortillas
- Oil
- Sea salt
- 1 tiny, onion (chopped)
- 2 cloves, ground garlic
- 1 1/2 lbs., ground sirloin
- 1, taco seasoning
- 1 15 oz, pinto beans

- 1 15 oz, corn
- 1 15 oz, tomatoes (diced)
- 1 cup, salsa
- 3 cups, chicken
- Sour cream & cheddar cheese (sliced)

Steps

1. Pour enough oil into a large, nonstick skillet to make it 1/6-1/4 Inches thick. There was a lot of stock in your house that you don't use. The liquid steams at moderate pressure. Place the tortillas in the air fryer and warm them up gradually. Allow them to cook until they bubble up and begin to color slightly. Then flip them over & cook for a couple of minutes more. Brush the tortillas with sea salt after removing them off a category implies with paper towels. Cook the tortillas till you've had your fill.
2. Over high-medium heat, bring a pot of soup to a boil. One tablespoon of oil is used. Combine the garlic & onion & sauté for 2 minutes, till the garlic is aromatic.
3. Season the taco with the seasoning and cook for about a minute.
4. Then there's the addition of beans, corn, salsa, tomatoes, and broth. Bring soup to a low boil, stirring constantly.
5. Reduce the heat to low and cover the soup to allow it to simmer gently. Allow the soup to simmer for at least 20 minutes before serving.
6. Serve the soup with fresh fried rice tortillas, grated cheese, & sour cream.

Nutritional Serving

357 Cal, Protein: 15 g, Carb: 10 g, Fat 1.3 g

2.38 Air Fryer Coconut Shrimp

Preparation Time: 10 mins

Cooking Time: 5 mins

Servings: 3

Ingredients

- 1/2-pound, big shrimp (uncooked)
- 1/2 cup, coconut (shredded)
- 3 tsp, panko breadcrumbs
- 2 big, egg whites
- 1/8 tsp, salt
- Pepper
- Hot sauce (Louisiana-style)
- 3 tsp, flour

for sauce

- 1/3 cup, Apricot
- 1/2 tsp, Vinegar
- red pepper flakes (Crushed)

Steps

1. Preheat an air fryer to 380°F. Shrimps are peeled and neatly diced while maintaining their tails.

2. In a small bowl, combine the coconut and breadcrumbs. In a separate small bowl, whisk together the salt, egg whites, pepper, & spicy sauce. Put flour in a shallow 3rd cup.

3. To coat the shrimp, carefully dip them in flour and brush off the excess. To help the coating adhere, dip it in the egg white combination & then pat it with the coconut mixture.

4. Arrange the shrimp in a single layer on the oiled plate in the air-fryer basket. Simmer for four minutes, then flip the shrimp and cook for four more minutes. Until the coconut has become a light golden-brown color and the shrimp has turned yellow.

5. In a small saucepan, combine the sauce ingredients; simmer and stir over medium-low heat till the preserves are dissolved. Serve the shrimp immediately with the sauce.

Nutritional Serving

250 Cal, Protein: 15 g, Carb: 30 g, Fat 9 g

2.39 Air Fryer Loaded Cheese & Onion Fries

Preparation Time: 10 mins

Cooking Time: 12 mins

Servings: 4

Ingredients

- 1/2 small, cucumber
- 1/2 tsp, salt
- 6 ounces, Greek yogurt
- 1 tbsp, lemon juice
- 2 tsp, dill (freeze & dried)
- 6 pieces, onion
- 1 tsp, garlic (minced)
- 1 tsp, vinegar
- 4 ounces, feta cheese box (crumbled)
- 4, russet potatoes
- 2 tsp, olive oil
- 2 tsp, Greek seasoning
- Cooking mist
- 1 tiny, red onion (sliced into strips)
- 1/4 cup, kalamata olives (sliced)
- 12, grape tomatoes (each halved)

Steps

1. In a sieve, shred the cucumber and season it with salt. Allow it to drain for 10 minutes.

2. In a small bowl, combine the dill, vinegar, milk, garlic, lemon juice, and feta to make the remainder of the tzatziki. Once everything is evenly blended, stir it again. When ready to use, stir in the cucumber (shredded) and set aside.
3. With an air fryer, heat to 450 degrees F.
4. Combine the fries, olive oil, & Greek spices in a large mixing bowl and toss until well combined. Coat the tray of air fryer with nonstick cooking spray. 1/2 of fries should be added to the basket.
5. In an air fryer, cook for 10 minutes. When done, flip and bake for another 5 minutes or so for the ideal crispness. Repeat with the remaining fries.
6. Divide the fries among four plates to serve. Drizzle cucumber sauce so over top of a fry. On each plate, marinate the olives, Kalamata olives, red onion strips, & grape tomatoes.

Nutritional Serving

453 Cal, Protein: 10 g, Carb: 17 g, Fat 0 g

2.40 Air Fryer Paneer Pakoras

Preparation Time: 15 mins

Cooking Time: 15 mins

Servings: 6

Ingredients

- 2 cups, cauliflower (sliced)
- 1 cup, potatoes (diced)
- Cheese
- 1 1/4 cups, chickpea flour
- 3/4 cup, water
- 1/2 tbsp red onion, (chopped)
- 1 tbsp, salt
- 1 clove, garlic
- 1 tsp, curry (powdered)
- 1 tsp, cilantro
- 1/2 tsp, cayenne pepper
- 1/2 tsp, cumin
- Cooking spray

Steps

1. Mix the potatoes, water, cauliflower, curry powder, cheese, cilantro, cayenne, red onion, chickpea flour, garlic, salt, & cumin together in a large mixing basin. Set aside 10 minutes to unwind.
2. Preheat the air fryer to 180°C.
3. Using the cooking spray, coat the air-fryer basket. Fill the basket halfway with the cauliflower mixture & smooth it out. Without disturbing the paneer pakoras, repeat the process.

4. Cook for another 8 mins on the other side. Place it on a platter that has been lined with towels. Rep with the remaining batter.

Nutritional Serving

50 Cal, Protein: 6.1 g, Carb: 0.3 g, Fat 6 g

2.41 Air Fryer Pork Balls

Preparation Time: 10 mins

Cooking Time: 20 mins

Servings: 12

Ingredients

- 2/3 cup, oats for quick cooking ()
- 1/2 cup, ritz crackers ()
- 2, eggs (beaten)
- 5 ounces, milk
- 1 tbsp, onion (minced)
- 1 tsp, salt
- 1 tsp, garlic
- 1 tsp, cumin ground
- 1 tsp, honey
- 1/2 tsp, mustard
- 2 pounds, pork

for Sauce

- 1/3 cup, brown sugar
- 1/3 cup, honey
- 1/3 cup, orange marmalade
- 2 tsp, cornstarch
- 2 tsp, soy sauce
- 1-2 tsp, hot sauce (Louisiana-style)
- 1 tbsp, Worcestershire sauce

Steps

1. Preheat the air fryer to 380 degrees. In a large mixing basin, combine the first 10 ingredients. Blend in the pork thoroughly but gently. Form 1-1/4-inch balls.

2. Place the pork balls in a single layer on an oiled tray inside an air-fryer basket. Cook for 14-15 mins, or until completely cooked and golden. Meanwhile, in a small pot, add the sauce ingredients. Over medium heat, cook & stir till it thickens.

Nutritional Serving

85 Cal, Protein: 6.1 g, Carb: 0.3 g, Fat: 6.7 g

2.42 Air Fryer Crab Cake

Preparation Time: 15 mins

Cooking Time: 10 mins

Servings: 4

Ingredients

- 8 ounces, Lamb crab meat
- ¼ cup, Almond flour
- 2 tbsp, fresh parsley (Chopped)

- 1, green onion
- ½ tsp, Old Bay seasoning
- ½ tsp, Salt
- ¼ tsp, Pepper
- 1, Egg
- 1 tbsp, Mayonnaise
- 2 tsp, Dijon mustard
- 2 tbsp, butter (Melted)

Steps

1. In a large mixing basin, break up "crab flesh" using a fork. In a large mixing bowl, combine the cinnamon, almond flour, pepper, parsley, green onion, & Old Bay.
2. Before the liquid is fully humidified, stir inside the mustard, mayonnaise, and egg. Form 4 patties with your hands, each approximately 3/4-1 inches thick. Chill for at least 30 mins on a platter lined with waxed paper.
3. Brush or spray the fryer rack with oil. Put crab cakes on the shelf after brushing both sides with melted butter.
4. At 350 degrees F, air fry for 10 minutes, gently flipping halfway through.
5. To make the mayonnaise, combine all of ingredients in a small cup.

Nutritional Serving

242 Cal, Protein: 28 g, Carb: 10.5 g, Fat: 9.4 g

2.43 Homemade Chicharrones, Pork Rind

Preparation Time: 25 mins

Cooking Time: 35 mins

Servings: 2

Ingredients

- 3-4 lb., pork skin & back fat
- Salt n pepper
- Cooking oil spray

Steps

1. Preheat oven to 250 degrees F & put a wire rack more than a baking sheet.
2. Using a sharp knife, cut your pork into thin strips about 2 inches wide. Each strip should be rated for fat every two inches. Put a knife between both the skin & the fat, place at a single end of strip and remove a portion of the fat.
3. While slipping the knife down strip to take most of the fat, maintain the skin inside one hand till the area of fat is extracted. It's OK if a little fat has already adhered to the muscle.
4. After fat has indeed been peeled, cut each strip into 2 inches squares and place fat-side down on wire shelf.
5. Preheat the oven to 350°F and bake for approximately 3 hours, or until the skin is dry.

6. Meanwhile, place the chicharrons in a large pan over medium heat if you wish to cook them with hog grease. Cook, stirring occasionally, for about 2 hours, or until most of fat has mixed with water. With a slotted spoon, scrape away any remaining solids. Dispose of (or feed; they have a bacon flavor and are great in salads)

7. While the baking time runs out, heat the oil/lard to a depth of about 1/3 in the pan. Alternatively, you may acquire a fraction of an inch of oil & make batches of pig rinds. It's intended that the oil would be warm but not boiling.

8. Cook for 3-5 mins, just until the pig rinds begin to boil and puff up. Remove to a category implies with towels and rinse. Season with salt n pepper right away.

Nutritional Serving

80 Kcal, Protein: 9 g, Carb: 0 g, Fat: 5 g

Chapter 3: Breakfast Recipes

3.1 Air Fryer Apple Fritters

Preparation Time: 10 mins

Cooking Time: 5 mins

Servings: 2

Ingredients

- Cooking spray
- 1 or 1/2 cups, flour
- 1 or 1/2 tsp, cinnamon
- 1/4 cup, sugar
- 1 tbsp, lemon juice
- 1/2 tsp, salt
- 2, eggs large
- 2 tsp, baking powder
- 2/3 cup, milk
- 2 medium, honey crisp apples (sliced)
- 1/4 cup, butter
- 1 cup, confectioners' sugar
- 1 tbsp, milk
- 1-1/2 tsp, vanilla extract

Steps

1. Preheat an air fryer to 410°F.
2. In a large mixing bowl, combine the salt, starch, baking powder, sugar, & cinnamon. Whisk together the remaining milk, eggs, lemon juice, and 1 teaspoon vanilla essence until the mixture is moistened. Fold the apples into the mixture.
3. Into each batch, drop 1/4 cup in dough. The air-fryer bowl has been removed. Spritz with frying spray. Cook for 5-6 minutes, or until golden brown. Flip the fritters and fry for another 1-2 minutes, or until lightly browned.
4. In a small saucepan, melt the butter over medium-high heat. Cook for 5 minutes, or until the butter & foam become a tan color. Remove from the heat and set aside to cool somewhat. Whisk together the browned butter, confectioners' sugar, milk, & 1/2 tsp vanilla extract till smooth. Drizzle over the fritters before serving.

Nutritional Serving

123 KCal, Protein: 2g, Carb: 3g, Fat: 4g

3.2 Air Fryer French Toast Sticks

Preparation Time: 10 mins

Cooking Time: 10 mins

Servings: 12

Ingredients

- 4, bread pieces
- 2, eggs
- 1 pinch, salt & cinnamon
- 1 pinch, nutmeg
- 1 tsp, icing sugar
- 2 tbsp, butter

Steps

1. Preheat the air fryer to 180 degrees Fahrenheit.
2. In a cup, lightly pound two eggs, a bit of salt, a few shakes of hard cinnamon, and small pinches both of nutmeg & crushed cloves.
3. Break the slices of bread into segments by buttering all sides.
4. Dredge the strips in egg mix & fried them inside an air fryer.
5. Stop the Air Fryer after 2 mins of frying, remove the oil, place it on a heat-safe surface, and coat the bread with nonstick spray.
6. Spray the second piece until all of the strips have been suitably sprayed.
7. Return pan to the fryer & cook for yet another 4 mins, checking after a few mins to make sure they're evenly cooked and not burned.
8. Remove from Air Fryer when the egg has been cooked, and the bread has been gently browned & consume right away.
9. For decoration and presentation, dust with icing sugar, top with ice cream, sprinkle over syrup, or symbolize a little dip cup of syrup.

Nutritional Serving

48 Cal, Protein: 1.9 g, Carb: 5 g, Fat: 2.2 g

3.3 Air Fryer Breakfast Toad-in-the-Hole Tarts

Preparation Time: 5 mins

Cooking Time: 25 mins

Servings: 4

Ingredients

- 1 sheet, puff pastry (frozen)
- 4 tbsp, cooked ham (sliced)
- 4 tbsp, cheddar cheese
- 1 tbsp, fresh chives (sliced)
- 4, eggs

Steps

1. For the air fryer, preheat to 400 degrees F.
2. Lay the pastry sheet out on a level surface and cut it into four squares.
3. Cook for 6-8 mins in the air fryer bowl with 2 pastry squares.
4. Take the air fryer out of the bowl and place it on a flat surface. Using a metal tablespoon, carefully push each square to create an oval shape. Put 1 tbsp. Cheddar cheese, 1 tbsp. ham, in every hole
5. Return to a air fryer with the basket in place. Cook for another 6 minutes, if required. Allow the tart to cool for 5 mins after removing it from the basket. Repeat with any remaining pastry squares, cheese, ham, and eggs.
6. Tarts garnished with chives

Nutritional Serving

446 Cal, Protein: 14 g, Carb: 27 g, Fat: 31 g

3.4 Air Fryer Churros

Preparation Time: 5 mins

Cooking Time: 15 mins

Servings: 6

Ingredients

- ¼ Cup, butter
- 1 pinch, salt
- ½ cup, milk
- 2 large, eggs
- ½ cup, flour
- ½ tsp, ground cinnamon
- ¼ cup, white sugar

Steps

1. In a saucepan, melt the butter over medium-high heat. Add a dash of milk and a pinch of salt. Reduce the heat to low and bring the water to a boil, stirring frequently with such a wooden spoon. All of the flour may be added at once. Continue to whisk until it is incorporated into the pastry.
2. Remove the pan from the heat and set it aside to cool for 5-7 mins. Before blending the pastry, beat the eggs with a wooden spoon. Fill a piping bag with the dough and a large star tip. Directly into the air fryer basket, pipe your dough into strips.
3. At 340 degrees F, air fry all churros for 5 minutes.
4. Meanwhile, mix the sugar & cinnamon in a small dish & spread over a deep plate.
5. Remove the cooked churros from air fryer & roll them in a cinnamon-sugar mixture.

Nutritional Serving

173 Cal, Protein: 3 g, Carb: 17 g, Fat: 9 g

3.5 Air Fryer Hard Boiled Eggs

Preparation Time: 15 mins

Cooking Time: 5 mins

Servings: 4

Ingredients

- 4, eggs

Steps

1. Preheat the air fryer to 250°F/120°C.
2. Place the wire rack in the air fryer basin and the eggs on top.
3. Cook for 16 minutes.
4. Remove the eggs from the air fryer and rapidly dunk them in icy water to stop the frying process.
5. Peel and let aside until completely cool.

Nutritional Serving

72 Cal, Protein: 6 g, Carb: 0 g, Fat: 5 g

3.6 Air Fryer Omelet

Preparation Time: 5 mins

Cooking Time: 5 mins

Servings: 1

Ingredients

- 1 pinch, salt
- ¼ cup, milk
- 2, eggs
- ¼ cup, shredded cheese
- 1 tsp, garden herb (breakfast seasoning)
- Meat & veggies (fresh)

Steps

1. In a small basin, whisk together the eggs & milk until well combined.
2. Add egg mixture to the pan, along with a pinch of salt.
3. Toss the veggies with the egg mixture.
4. Pour the egg mixture into a greased 6"x3" pan.
5. Put the pan in the basket of the air fryer.
6. Preheat oven to 350 degrees Fahrenheit and bake for 8-10 minutes.
7. Sprinkle breakfast seasoning over the eggs and the cheese over the top halfway through the cooking process.
8. With a narrow spatula, soften the omelet from pan's sides and transfer it to a plate.

Nutritional Serving

156 Cal, Protein: 13 g, Carb: 7 g, Fat: 9 g

3.7 Air Fryer McDonald's Copycat Egg McMuffin

Preparation Time: 10 mins

Cooking Time: 5 mins

Servings: 2

Ingredients

- 2, eggs
- 2. Muffins
- 2 slices, bacon
- 2 slices, cheese

Steps

1. Preheat the air fryer to 400 degrees Fahrenheit.
2. Cover the rack with foil.
3. Spray the pan with cooking oil.
4. In each jar cover, crack one egg.
5. Arrange the bacon on rack.
6. Heat for 5 minutes, rotating the bacon halfway through.
7. Cook for a further 5 minutes.
8. Remove the eggs.
9. Bake the sliced muffins in air fryer for 5 minutes, or until light golden.
10. Place a slice of cheese, bacon, and an egg on the muffin.

Nutritional Serving

666 Cal, Protein: 22 g, Carb: 21 g, Fat: 23 g

3.8 Air Fryer Breakfast Pizza

Preparation Time: 15 mins

Cooking Time: 35 mins

Servings: 16

Ingredients

- Crescent dough
- 3, eggs (scrambled)
- Sausage (crumbled)
- ½, pepper (minced)
- 1/2 cup, cheddar cheese
- 1/2 cup, mozzarella cheese

Steps

1. Pour some oil into the pan.
2. In the bottom layer of a pan, spread out the dough.
3. Preheat the air fryer to 350 degrees for 5 minutes, or until the top layer is gently toasted.
4. Remove the air fryer from the oven.
5. Sausage, cheese, peppers, & eggs are layered on top.
6. Set the air fryer for a further 5-10 minutes.

Nutritional Serving

313 Cal, Protein: 13 g, Carb: 12 g, Fat: 21 g

3.9 Air Fryer Cherry and Cream Cheese Danish

Preparation Time: 10 mins

Cooking Time: 10 mins

Servings: 8

Ingredients

- Icing
- Rolls Dough Pillsbury Crescent
- 8 oz, Cream Cheese
- 16 oz, Cherry Pie Filling

Steps

1. Preheat the air fryer to 350°F.
2. I wrapped the crescent dough with plastic wrap.
3. Wrap the very top layer once again. Fill each roll in cream cheese & compress the edges to form a circle.
4. On a rack, place an air fryer.
5. Preheat oven to 390°F for 10 minutes.
6. The top layer will become a light brown color.
7. Place foil on top of a tray & cook for a further 10 minutes.
8. Remove it from the oven and ice it.

Nutritional Serving

239 Cal, Protein: 4 g, Carb: 30 g, Fat: 12 g

3.10 Air-Fryer Southern Cheese

Preparation Time: 1 min

Cooking Time: 10 mins

Servings: 1

Ingredients

- 2 slices, bread
- 2, eggs
- 3-4 pieces, bacon
- 1 tbsp, mayonnaise
- ½-1 tbsp, butter

Steps

1. Put 3 to 4 pieces of bacon inside an air fryer at high heat, roughly 375-390 degrees.
2. Cook bacon approximately 3 mins or until it reaches your desired crispiness.
3. A medium-hot pan, butter, & slightly toasted piece of bread should be set aside.
4. In a pan, fry two eggs and make the sandwiches bread to order.
5. Flip your egg halfway through cooking to ensure even cooking on both sides.

6. Before transferring the fried egg on the toasted crust, place one piece of cheese on top.
7. After that, add air-fried, crispy bacon to a poached egg with cheese.
8. Put the second piece of cheese on top of a bacon, then other slice of bread (toasted) to finish the sandwich.
9. Finally, set breakfast sandwich in air fryer for one to two minutes to toast it and make it nice, sweet, and crispy.
10. Remove the frozen food from the freezer.

Nutritional Serving

370 Cal, Protein: 23 g, Carb: 30 g, Fat: 17 g

3.11 Air-Fried Breakfast Bombs

Preparation Time: 20 mins

Cooking Time: 5 mins

Servings: 2

Ingredients

- 3 slices, bacon
- 3 large, eggs
- 1 tbsp, fresh chives
- 1-ounce, cream cheese
- Oil spray
- 4-ounces, wheat pizza dough

Steps

1. In a small pan, cook the bacon until it is somewhat crisp, about 10 minutes. Remove the bacon from the pan and crumble it. Cook, continually stirring, for about 1 minute, until the eggs are nearly hard but still loose in the pan with the bacon drippings. In a mixing dish, combine the eggs, cream cheese, chives, and crumbled bacon.
2. Cut dough into 4 pieces that are all the same size. On a lightly floured, roll each piece into a 5-inch circle. In the middle of each dough circle, put a quarter of egg mixture. Clean the dough's outside border with water; make a purse out of the dough by tying it around egg mixture & pinching the seams together.
3. Place dough purses in a single layer into air fryer baskets and coat with cooking spray. Cook at 350°F for 5–6 minutes, or till golden brown, monitoring after 5 mins.

Nutritional Serving

305 Cal, Protein: 19 g, Carb: 26 g, Fat: 15 g

3.12 Air Fryer Biscuit Breakfast Bombs

Preparation Time: 35 mins

Cooking Time: 10 mins

Servings: 8

Ingredients

- 1 tbsp, vegetable oil
- ¼ lb., bulk breakfast sausage
- 2, eggs
- 1/8 tsp, salt
- 1/8 tsp, pepper
- Biscuits bomb
- 1 can, Pillsbury
- 2 oz, cheddar cheese
- 1 tbsp, egg wash & water

Steps

1. Make two 8-inch circles out of the cooking parchment paper. Place one round in the bottom of air fryer basket.

2. In a 10 inches nonstick skillet, heat the oil over middle to high heat. Cook the sausages in the oil for 2-5 mins, till it is no longer pink, tossing regularly to crumble; transfer to the a medium basin with a wooden spoon. Reduce the heat to a medium setting. Add crushed eggs, salt, & pepper to pan drippings; simmer, often turning, till eggs are thickened but still wet. In a cup, whisk up the eggs and pour them over the sausage. Allow for five minutes of cooling time.

3. Meanwhile, split the dough into 5 biscuits and layer each one twice. Make each one into a 4-inch circle. Place one in the center of every circular heaped tablespoonful of egg mixture. One of cheese chunks should be placed on top of it. Carefully fold the edges up & over the filling, pressing to seal. In a shallow cup, whisk together the majority of the egg & water. Both ends of the biscuits should be rubbed with egg wash.

4. Place 5 biscuit bombs seam side down on the paper in the air fryer dish. Water the second ring of parchment on both sides with the cooking water. Cover the remaining 5 biscuit bombs in the dish with the second parchment round biscuit bombs.

5. Preheat oven to 325°F and bake for 8 minutes. Remove the round parchment and gently turn the cookies into a single layer in the basket using tongs. Heat for another 4 to 6 minutes or until cooked through (at least 165° F).

Nutritional Serving

156 Cal, Protein: 4 g, Carb: 10 g, Fat: 9 g

3.13 Air Fryer Stuffed Breakfast Bombs with Eggs & Bacon

Preparation Time: 35 mins

Cooking Time: 15 mins

Servings: 10

Ingredients

- ½ cup, Bacon
- 1 cup, Eggs
- ½ cup, Cheddar cheese
- Salt n pepper
- 1 package, Freeze biscuits

Steps

1. In a small bowl, combine the poached eggs, baked bacon, & melted Cheddar cheese.
2. Toss a few tablespoons of the mixture into the biscuit and place it in the center.
3. Simply cover the biscuit with another biscuit, wrap it around itself, and press hard to conceal the edges. Place the air fryer dish in the air fryer.
4. Preheat the air fryer to 320 degrees Fahrenheit and cook for 5 minutes.
5. Take a seat at the table, eat, and relax.

Nutritional Serving

160 Cal, Protein: 5 g, Carb: 14 g, Fat: 9 g

3.14 Air Fryer Breakfast Burritos

Preparation Time: 40 mins

Cooking Time: 10 mins

Servings: 7

Ingredients

- ½ Lb., ground sausage
- 1/3 cup, bacon bits
- ½, bell pepper
- ½ cup, cheese (shredded)
- Spraying oil
- 6 medium, flour tortillas
- 6, eggs

Steps

1. Combine the sausage (fried), eggs (scrambled), bacon pieces, bell pepper, and cheese in a large mixing dish. To combine the ingredients, stir them together.
2. Fill each flour tortilla core with approximately half a cup of the mixture.
3. After that, fold the ends and move.
4. Rep with the remaining ingredients.

5. Fill the air fryer basket with filled burritos and generously spray with oil.
6. Preheat the oven to 330°f and cook for 5 minutes.

Nutritional Serving

534 Cal, Protein: 27 g, Carb: 34 g, Fat: 32 g

3.15 Air Fryer Breakfast Frittata

Preparation Time: 15 mins

Cooking Time: 20 mins

Servings: 2

Ingredients

- ½ Cup, cheddar cheese
- ¼ pound, breakfast sausage
- 4 large, eggs
- 2 tbsp, red bell pepper
- 1, green onion
- 1 pinch, cayenne pepper
- Cooking spray

Steps

1. In a mixing dish, combine all the ingredients.
2. Preheat the air fryer to 360°F.
3. Place the ingredients in a cake pan that has previously been prepared.
4. Cook for 19-20 minutes, or until the frittata is adjusted.

Nutritional Serving

380 Cal, Protein: 31 g, Carb: 2 g, Fat: 27 g

3.16 Air Fryer Crispy Bacon

Preparation Time: 5 mins

Cooking Time: 15 mins

Servings: 6

Ingredients

- ¾ lb., one bacon (Thick)

Steps

1. Place a thin layer of bacon on the bottom of the air fryer.
2. Preheat an air fryer to 400°F & cook for 8-10 minutes, or until crispy.

Nutritional Serving

67 Cal, Protein: 4 g, Carb: 0.2 g, Fat: 5.4 g

3.17 Air Fryer Raspberry Muffins

Preparation Time: 10 mins

Cooking Time: 15 mins

Servings: 3

Ingredients

- 1 tsp, baking powder
- 1 cup, flour
- ½ tsp, orange zest
- 1/3 cup, sugar

- 1/3 cup, milk
- 1, egg
- 2.5 tbsp, vegetable oil
- 1/8 tsp, salt
- ½ tsp, vanilla essence
- ½ tbsp, raw vanilla sugar
- ½ cup, raspberries

Steps

1. In the muffin pan, place a muffin paper.
2. In a mixing basin, combine the baking powder, salt, & flour.
3. In a separate dish, thoroughly combine the sugar, egg, vanilla, & milk.
4. Combine the wet and dry ingredients in a bowl and gently cover with raspberries.
5. Divide the muffin batter into muffin cups with a vanilla sugar surface coating.
6. Bake for 15 minutes inside an air fryer until the muffins are done. Set them aside to allow them to cool down thoroughly.

Nutritional Serving

253 Cal, Protein: 5 g, Carb: 37 g, Fat: 9 g

3.18 Air Fryer Tofu

Preparation Time: 10 mins

Cooking Time: 5 mins

Servings: 2

Ingredients

- 2 tbsp, soy sauce
- 453 g, black firm tofu
- 1 tbsp, olive oil
- 1 tbsp, sesame oil
- 1 clove, garlic

Steps

1. Using a firm pan or laying it on top, press the tofu by at least seven minutes to allow the liquid to drain out. When the tofu is done, it is chopped into bite-sized bits and placed in a serving plate.
2. Combine all the leftover ingredients in a small cup. Drizzle over the tofu and toss to coat. Allow the tofu to marinate for another 15 minutes.
3. Preheat the air fryer to 190°C. Add tofu blocks to air Fryer bowl in a single layer. Cook for 15 mins, shaking the pan often to aid frying. Allow the muffins to cool slightly in the baking pan before transferring them to a cooling rack.

Nutritional Serving

143 Cal, Protein: 9 g, Carb: 2 g, Fat: 11 g

3.19 Air Fryer Brussel Sprouts

Preparation Time: 45 mins

Cooking Time: 15 mins

Servings: 8

Ingredients

- 1 pound, Brussel sprouts
- 1 tbsp, olive oil
- 1 medium, shallot
- ½ tsp, salt
- 2 tbsp, butter (unsalted)
- 1 tsp, red wine vinegar

Steps

1. Preheat an air fryer to 375 degrees Fahrenheit. Next, cut a pound of Brussels sprouts into halves, halving any sprouts that are longer than just an inch across. In a medium mixing bowl, combine 1 tablespoon olive oil & 1/2 tsp kosher salt.

2. Add Brussels sprouts to the air fryer and mix them together onto a single platter. For a total of fifteen min, air fry, pausing to turn the bowl around halfway through. Meanwhile, start making the shallot butter.

3. 1 medium shallot, finely chopped, 2 tablespoons unsalted butter inside a large microwave-safe dish, heated in the microwave Mix in the shallots & 1 tsp red wine vinegar until everything is well combined.

4. When the Brussel sprout are done, combine them with shallot butter in a mixing basin or saucepan. Serve right away.

Nutritional Serving

45 Cal, Protein: 2 g, Carb: 9 g, Fat: 0 g

Chapter 4: Lunch Recipes

4.1 Air Fryer Donuts

Preparation Time: 15 mins

Cooking Time: 10 mins

Servings: 4

Ingredients

- 1 cup, milk
- ½ tsp, instant yeast 2.
- ¼ cup, sugar
- ½ tsp, salt
- 1, egg
- ¼ cup, butter
- 3 cups, flour
- Oil spray

Steps

1. In the stand mixer fitted with a dough handle, stir together milk, 1 teaspoon sugar, and yeast. Allow it to sit for 10 minutes, or until it foams up.
2. Add the sugar, egg, & cinnamon, as well as the butter (melted) and 2 cups of flour, to the milk mixture. Mix on low until well combined, then gradually add the cup of flour while the mixer is running, till the dough never longer adheres to the pipe. Increase the speed to medium-low & knead for 5 minutes, or till the dough is elastic & smooth.
3. In an oiled bowl, place the dough & cover this with plastic wrap. Allow it to develop in a warm location before it doubles in size.
4. Put the dough on a surface (floured), punch it down, & stretch it out to about 1/2 inch thickness. 1- To get the center out, cut 11-13 doughnuts in half.
5. Replace the parchment paper donuts & doughnut holes with lightly floured parchment-lined donuts & donut holes, & cover loosely in oiled plastic wrap. Allow for a 30-minute growth period before doubling the number of doughnuts. Preheat the Air Fryer to 350°F.
6. Spray the Fryer bowl with the oil spray & carefully transfer the doughnuts to the Fryer jar in a single layer. Spray doughnuts with oil spray and bake at 350°F for 4 minutes, or until golden brown. Rep for the remaining donuts and gaps.

7. When the donuts are now in the Air Fryer, melt butter in a small saucepan over medium heat. Until smooth, stir in the sugar & vanilla extract powder. Remove from the stove and stir in one tablespoon of hot water at a time till the icing is thin but not runny.

8. Dip hot donuts & doughnut holes into glaze with forks to fully soak them. Place it on a wire rack over a baking sheet (rimmed) to allow excess glaze to drip off. Before the glaze solidifies, let it stand for approximately 10 minutes.

Nutritional Serving

128 Cal, Protein: 21 g, Carb: 3 g, Fat 8 g

4.2 Bang Bang Chicken

Preparation Time: 15 mins

Cooking Time: 10 mins

Servings: 8

Ingredients

- 1/2 cup, Mayonnaise
- 2 tbsp, Honey
- 1/2 tbsp, Sriracha sauce
- 1 cup, Buttermilk
- ¾, Flour
- ½ cup, Cornstarch
- 1, Egg
- Oil

Steps

1. To make bang chicken sauce, merge all ingredients inside a mixing basin. Before you combine anything, whisk everything together.

2. To make bang bang meat inside the air fryer, combine flour, eggs, corn starch, salt, Pepper, sriracha sauce, & Buttermilk in a mixing bowl. And stir until everything is nicely combined.

3. Oil your Fryer with the oil of your choice before adding the chicken. After that, work in batches, dipping portions of chicken into buttermilk batter & coating the Air Fryer with breadcrumbs. Air 8-10 minutes at 375°F or till chicken is cooked through. Rotate the chicken chunks, on the other hand.

4. Serve with leafy greens/Eggs & Green Onion Spanish Rice Recipe after drizzling the sauce over the chicken.

Nutritional Serving

514 Cal, Protein: 21 g, Carb: 23 g, Fat 10 g

4.3 Crispy Air Fryer Eggplant Parmesan

Preparation Time: 10 mins

Cooking Time: 20 mins

Servings: 6

Ingredients

- 1 large, Eggplant
- ½ cup, Wheat breadcrumbs
- 3 tbsp, Parmesan cheese
- Salt
- 1 tsp, Italian seasoning
- 3 tbsp, Flour
- 1 tbsp, Water
- Olive oil spray
- 1 cup. Marinara sauce
- ¼ cup. Mozzarella cheese
- Fresh parsley

Steps

1. "Cut the eggplant into 1/2-inch-thick pieces." Season both ends of slices with salt and let aside for 10-15 minutes.
2. In a small bowl, whisk together the egg, water, and flour to produce the batter.
3. In a large shallow bowl, combine the cheese, salt, Italian seasoning, & breadcrumbs. Make a thorough mix.
4. Now evenly distribute the batter among the eggplant slices. Add battered halves to the breadcrumb mixture to evenly coat all sides.
5. Place breaded eggplant slices on a clean, dry flat dish and drizzle with oil.
6. Preheat the Fryer to 360 degrees Fahrenheit. Place the eggplant slices just on wire mesh & cook for about 8 minutes.
7. Cover air-fried pieces with about 1 tablespoon of marinara sauce & fresh mozzarella thinly distributed on top. Cook for another 2 minutes, or until the cheese has melted.
8. Serve gently on the side of your favorite spaghetti.

Nutritional Serving

122 Cal, Protein: 80 g, Carb: 45 g, Fat 22 g

4.4 Air Fryer Shrimp Fajitas

Preparation Time: 30 mins

Cooking Time: 15 mins

Servings: 7

Ingredients

- 1-pound, medium shrimp
- 1, red bell pepper
- 1, green bell pepper
- 1/2 cup, sweet onion
- 2 tbsp, gluten-free fajita
- Olive oil spray
- Flour tortillas or white corn tortillas

Steps

1. Just on-air fryer basin, spray little olive oil, and cover with foil.
2. If shrimp is trapped with ice on it, run cold water around it to remove it.
3. Toss together the tomatoes, seafood, spice, and cabbage in a mixing dish.
4. Mist a layer with olive oil to adhere it.
5. Toss everything together.
6. Using Ninja Foody Air Fryer, cook for 12 mins at 390 degrees.
7. Open the cap and sprinkle it all over again, blending it all together.
8. Cook for another 10 minutes.
9. Eat on soft tortillas.

Nutritional Serving

140 Cal, Protein: 85 g, Carb: 40 g, Fat 30 g

4.5 Honey Glazed Air Fryer Salmon

Preparation Time: 15 mins

Cooking Time: 15 mins

Servings: 2

Ingredients

- 4, Salmon Fillets
- Salt
- Black Pepper
- 2 tsp, Soy Sauce
- 1 tbsp, Honey
- 1 tsp, Sesame Seeds

Steps

1. Preheat your air fryer (it takes 1 to 2 minutes).

2. Additionally, season each salmon fillet with pepper and salt. Soy sauce should be applied to the fish.

3. Place the fillets in air fryer's bowl & cook at 375°F (190°C) for 8 mins or till done.

4. Glaze each fillet with honey for a min or two till the timer goes off, then sprinkle sesame seeds on top. Take them back into it to complete the cooking.

5. Serve with a dish of your choice.

Nutritional Serving

136 Cal, Protein: 90 g, Carb: 39 g, Fat 17 g

4.6 Crispy Air Fryer Roasted Brussels Sprouts With Balsamic

Preparation Time: 15 mins

Cooking Time: 15 mins

Servings: 8

Ingredients

- 1 pound, Brussels sprouts
- 2 tbsp, Olive oil
- 1 tbsp, Balsamic vinegar
- Salt
- Black Pepper

Steps

1. In a dish, place the chopped sprouts. Toss the Brussels sprouts with a large amount of vinegar and oil. Don't mix the vinegar & oil in one spot, and don't simply brush one of Brussels sprouts.

2. Season the Brussels sprouts liberally with pepper and salt. Mix well to integrate all of the ingredients and for long enough for the marinade to soak up all of the Brussels sprouts.

3. Place the Brussels in the air fryer's bowl. Fry the air at 359°F for around 15-20 minutes. Cook for approximately 7-8 minutes, shaking and carefully stirring midway through. Make sure shaking is still going at the midway point. If required, shake and rotate it a third time to ensure that it cooks evenly.

4. Attempt to thoroughly air-fry Brussels for the remainder of the session. If necessary, search sooner to ensure that nothing burns.

5. Season the Brussels sprouts with more salt and pepper if desired, and serve.

Nutritional Serving

129 Cal, Protein: 25 g, Carb: 30 g, Fat 14 g

4.7 Air Fryer Chicken Nuggets

Preparation Time: 20 mins

Cooking Time: 15 mins

Servings: 8

Ingredients

- Cooking spray
- 2, Chicken breasts
- 1/3 cup, Olive oil
- 1.5 cup, Panko
- ¼ cup, Parmesan
- 2 tsp, Sweet paprika

Steps

1. Set up the station with one dish containing olive oil and the other having panko, parmesan, & paprika, then break your chicken breasts into 1" to 1.5" cubes and set them aside.
2. Using a spritzer, lightly lubricate the inside of your air fryer.
3. Place the chicken cube on top of the suit after dipping it in olive oil. Put the nugget in air fryer after making sure it's well-coated. On your air fryer, repeat till it's finished.
4. Cook homemade chicken nuggets in an air fryer at 400°F for 8 minutes.
5. Accompany with your preferred side dish.

Nutritional Serving

156 Cal, Protein: 85 g, Carb: 25 g, Fat 14 g

4.8 Air Fryer Baked Apples

Preparation Time: 15 mins

Cooking Time: 15 mins

Servings: 12

Ingredients

- 2, apples
- 1 tsp, butter
- ½ tsp, cinnamon

Steps

1. Break chicken breasts into 1" to 1.5" pieces and set aside.
2. Set up the station with one dish containing olive oil and the other with parmesan, paprika mixture, and panko.
3. Using some oil, lightly spray the inside of your air fryer.
4. Place the chicken cube on top of suit after dipping it in olive oil. Make sure the nugget is well-coated before placing it in air fryer. Continue until your air fryer is empty.
5. Preheat the air fryer to 400°f and cook homemade chicken nuggets for 8 minutes.
6. Serve with a side dish of your choice.

Nutritional Serving

147 Cal, Protein: 36 g, Carb: 5 g, Fat 0 g

4.9 Air Fryer Fish Tacos

Preparation Time: 15 mins

Cooking Time: 10 mins

Servings: 6

Ingredients

- 24 oz, Firm white fish fillets
- 1 tbsp, Grill seasoning
- 1 large, Avocado
- 2, Oranges (medium)
- 1/4 cup, Red onion
- 2 tbsp, fresh cilantro
- 1 tsp, Salt
- 1/4 cup, Mayonnaise
- 1/4 cup, Chipotle sauce
- 1 tbsp, Lime juice
- Corn tortillas

Steps

1. Combine the orange, avocado, coriander, cilantro, & 1/2 teaspoon of salt in a mixing bowl.
2. Combine the chipotle sauce, mayo, lime juice, & 1/2 teaspoon salt in a mixing bowl.
3. Season the fish liberally with grill seasoning.
4. Spray air-fryer basket with the vegetable oil to prevent sticking.
5. Arrange the fish in a single strip in the bowl. Cook for 8-12 mins at 400°F, or until the internal temperature of the salmon reaches 145°F. It is not necessary to flip the fish throughout the frying process.
6. To create tacos, combine the fish, avocado (warmed), citrus salsa, corn tortillas, & chipotle mayonnaise in a mixing bowl.

Nutritional Serving

129 Cal, Protein: 25 g, Carb: 30 g, Fat 14 g

4.10 Air Fryer Dumplings

Preparation Time: 20 mins

Cooking Time: 15 mins

Servings: 6

Ingredients

- 8 ounces, Chicken dumplings
- 1/4 cup, Soy sauce
- 1/4 cup, Water
- 1/8 cup, Maple syrup
- 1/2 tsp, Garlic powder
- 1/2 tsp, Rice vinegar

- red pepper flakes (Small pinch)

Steps

1. Preheat air fryer to 370 degrees for around 4 minutes.
2. Spray the frozen dumplings with gasoline and arrange them in a single layer in the air fryer.
3. Fry for 5 mins, then flip the bowl and spray with a little extra oil.
4. Cook the dumplings for another 4-6 minutes.
5. In the meanwhile, combine the ingredients for the dipping sauce.
6. Remove the fried dumpling from of the dish and set aside for another 2 mins before eating.

Nutritional Serving

514 Cal, Protein: 21 g, Carb: 23 g, Fat 10 g

4.11 Air Fryer Pork Special Chops

Preparation Time: 20 mins

Cooking Time: 15 mins

Servings: 6

Ingredients

- 4 chops, pork (Boneless)
- 1 tbsp, Grill seasoning
- 1/4 cup, Maple syrup
- 2 tbsp, Dijon mustard
- 2 tsp, Lemon juice
- 1/2 tsp, Salt
- Vegetable oil

Steps

1. Vegetable oil should be gently rubbed into the air-fryer basket.
2. Clean the pork chops with paper towels and thoroughly season both sides with the barbecue spice.
3. In the air fryer basket, arrange pork chops in a single layer. Depending on the size of your air fryer, you may need to bake pork chops in 2 batches.
4. Preheat the oven to 375°F and bake the pork chops for 12 to 15 minutes. Turn the pork chops halfway through the cooking period.
5. When the pork chops have reached an internal temperature of 145 degrees F, they are done frying.
6. While a pork chops are cooking, combine the maple syrup, lemon juice, , & salt in an air fryer.
7. Immediately after removing the pork chops from air fryer, pour the sauce over them.

8. Allow pork chops to rest for 2 mins before serving.

Nutritional Serving

160 Cal, Protein: 20 g, Carb: 11 g, Fat 1 g

4.12 Air Fryer Chicken Chimichangas

Preparation Time: 25 mins

Cooking Time: 15 mins

Servings: 10

Ingredients

- 1, white meat Rotisserie chicken
- 1 1/2 cups, Cooked rice
- 1 cup, Salsa
- 1/2 tsp, Salt
- 8 inches, Soft taco flour tortillas
- 2 tbsp, Vegetable oil

Steps

1. For the air fryer, coat the bottom of a basket with vegetable oil. Preheat the air fryer to 360 degrees Fahrenheit.
2. In a large mixing bowl, combine the salt, chicken, rice, & salsa.
3. Place approximately 1/2 cup of chicken filling in the center of each tortilla. Wrap the ends securely around the lining, bent in to seal it in.
4. Put the chimichangas in greased bowl, seam side down, two at a time. Clean the tops of chimichangas carefully with vegetable oil.
5. Chimichangas should be air-fried for around 4 mins at 360 degrees. Start an air fryer & use metal tongs to turn the chimichangas. Continue to air-fried the chimichangas for another 4 mins after they are crispy and golden.
6. The filling will be kept in an airtight container in the refrigerator for up to two days so that the chimichangas may be made as desired.
7. On top of the chimichangas, spread sour garlic, white cheese sauce, onion, spinach, & guacamole.

Nutritional Serving

170 Cal, Protein: 125 g, Carb: 95 g, Fat 25 g

4.13 Simple Chicken Burrito Bowls

Preparation Time: 10 mins

Cooking Time: 5 mins

Servings: 10

Ingredients

- 1, rotisserie chicken
- 1 15 oz, black beans
- 1 15 oz, corn

- 1 8 oz packet, taco skillet sauce
- 1 tbsp, vegetable oil
- 1 cup, white rice
- 1 tsp, salt
- 1 3/4 cup, water
- 2 tbsp, taco sauce
- 1 cup, iceberg lettuce
- 1, avocado
- 4, lime wedges
- 6 oz, medium cheddar cheese
- ½ cup, sour cream
- 4 oz, jalapenos

Steps

1. In a large saucepan, combine the black beans, chicken, taco skillet sauce, & corn. Over medium-low heat, combine all ingredients, cover, and cook until simmering.

2. Meanwhile, in a separate saucepan, heat the oil over medium-high pressure. Before the rice starts to toast, add it and simmer for a minute, stirring occasionally. Bring the sauce to a boil with the water, salt, and taco. Cover and cook for 15-20 minutes, or until all of the water has been absorbed. Reduce the amount of pressure.

3. Fill the cups with a generous scoop of rice, then top with the meat, beans, and maize combination. Optional ingredients include a lime wedge, chopped avocado, shredded lettuce, cheese (shredded), sliced jalapenos, and sour cream. Serve right away.

Nutritional Serving

150 Cal, Protein: 95 g, Carb: 40 g, Fat: 22 g

4.14 Chicken Soft Tacos

Preparation Time: 15 mins

Cooking Time: 5 mins

Servings: 6

Ingredients

- 3 tbsp, butter (unsalted)
- 4 cloves, garlic
- 2 tsp, chipotle chiles
- 1/2 cup, orange
- 1/2 cup, Worcestershire sauce
- 3/4 cup, cilantro
- 4, chicken breasts (boneless & skinless)
- 1 tsp, yellow mustard
- Salt n pepper
- 12 4-inch, flour tortillas

Steps

1. Melt the butter in a large pan over medium-high heat.

2. Roast for about 1 minute, or until the garlic & chipotle are aromatic.
3. Bring to a boil with the Worcestershire sauce, orange juice, & 1/2 cup cilantro.
4. Add the chicken and simmer for 10 to 15 minutes, covered, over medium-low heat, until the flesh is 160 degrees, turning halfway through. Transfer to the foil-plate & set up a tent.
5. Raise the heat and add & continue to cook for about 5 minutes, or until the liquid has been decreased to 1/4 cup.
6. Off the heat, whisk in the mustard.
7. Return the chicken to the pan after shredding it with two forks into bite-sized pieces.
8. Add the remaining cilantro to a saucepan and stir until completely combined. Season with salt and pepper.
9. Garnish with lime wedges, shredded cabbage, tortillas, salsa, cheese, and sour cream.

Nutritional Serving

156 Cal, Protein: 90 g, Carb: 44 g, Fat 20 g

4.15 Ground Pork Tacos - Al Pastor Style

Preparation Time: 10 mins

Cooking Time: 10 mins

Servings: 6

Ingredients

- 1 1/3 lbs., Pork
- 1/3 cup, Orange
- 3 tbsp, chipotle sauce (Canned)
- 1 tsp, Smoked paprika
- 1 tsp, Cumin
- 1 tsp, Salt
- 1/2 tsp, Garlic powder
- 1/4 tsp, Cayenne Pepper
- 1 1/2 cups, Pineapple
- 1/3 cup, finely diced Red onion
- 1/3 cup, Cilantro
- ½, Juice of lime
- 1/2 tsp, Salt
- 6 oz, Pepper Jack cheese
- Corn tortillas

Steps

1. Set aside the cilantro, pineapple, lime juice, red onion, & 1/2 teaspoon in a bowl.
2. In a nonstick pan over medium heat, add the diced pork and cook until it is no longer, cutting ties with a spatula.
3. In a mixing bowl, combine the chipotle sauce, orange juice, paprika (smoked), garlic powder, cumin, & the remaining tsp

of cayenne pepper. Allow for a 5-minute simmer after stirring well.

4. On the pork taco meat, serve with tortillas, pineapple salsa (organic), & sliced Pepper Jack cheese.

Nutritional Serving

190 Cal, Protein: 96 g, Carb: 45 g, fat 15 g

4.16 Air-Fryer Southern-Style Chicken

Preparation Time: 20 mins

Cooking Time: 15 mins

Servings: 6

Ingredients

- 2 cups, Ritz crackers (Crushed)
- 1 tbsp, Fresh parsley
- 1 tsp, Garlic salt
- 1 tsp, Paprika
- 1/2 tsp, Pepper
- 1/4 tsp, Cumin
- 1/4 tsp, Rubbed sage
- 1, large Egg
- 1, fryer/broiler chicken
- Cooking spray

Steps

1. Preheat an air fryer to 375 degrees. In a small mixing bowl, combine the first seven ingredients. In a separate shallow dish, crack the egg. To help the chicken stick to the coating, dip it in the shell and then pat it with the cracker mixture. Sprinkle the cooking mist over chicken in the batches and place it on the greased tray in air-fryer bowl.

2. Cook for 10 mins before serving. Transform the spritz & chicken with cooking oil; cook till the chicken is golden brown and the juices are clear, about 15-20 minutes more.

Nutritional Serving

200 Cal, Protein: 100 g, Carb: 70 g, Fat 30 g

4.17 Air-Fryer Fish & Fries

Preparation Time: 60 mins

Cooking Time: 20 mins

Servings: 10

Ingredients

- 1 pound, potatoes
- 2 tbsp, olive oil
- 1/4 tsp, Pepper
- 1/4 tsp, salt

For fish:

- 1/3 cup, flour
- 1/4 tsp, Pepper
- 1 large, egg
- 2 tbsp, water
- 2/3 cup, cornflakes
- 1 tbsp, parmesan cheese
- 1/8 tsp, cayenne Pepper
- 1/4 tsp, salt
- 1 pound, haddock

Steps

1. Preheat the air fryer to 400 degrees. Peel & cut the potatoes lengthwise into 1/2-inch-thick slices, then cut the pieces into 1/2-inch-thick sticks.

2. In a large mixing basin, toss potatoes with the oil, pepper, and salt. Place potatoes just on air-fryer basket tray in batches inside a single layer; heat until just soft, 5-10 mins to redistribute tossing potatoes; cook till slightly golden brown & crisp, 5-10 mins more.

3. Meanwhile, in a separate dish, mix the flour and pepper. In a separate small bowl, whisk together the egg and water. In a third bowl, combine the cornflakes, cheese, and cayenne. Season the fish with salt, then dip it in flour mixture to cover both sides & brush off the excess. Dip in the shell mixture, then pat in cornflake mixture to help it stick to the coating.

4. Remove the fries from the bowl and keep them heated. Arrange fish in a thin layer on plate in an air-fryer bowl. Cook until the fish is lightly browned and only starts to break easily with such a fork after 9 minutes of cooking, flipping halfway through. Do not continue to overcook it. Put the fries to basket to reheat. Serve right away. If required, provide with tartar sauce.

Nutritional Serving

180 Cal, Protein: 89 g, Carb: 40 g, Fat 15 g

4.18 Air-Fryer Ground Beef Wellington

Preparation Time: 20 mins

Cooking Time: 10 mins

Servings: 6

Ingredients

- 1 tbsp, butter
- 1/2 cup, mushrooms
- 2 tsp, flour
- 1/4 tsp, Pepper
- 1/2 cup, half & half cream
- 1 large, egg yolk
- 2 tbsp, onion

- 1/4 tsp, salt
- 1/2-pound, beef
- 4 ounces, freeze crescent rolls (1 tube)
- 1, large egg
- 1 tsp, parsley flakes

Steps

1. Preheat the air fryer to 300 degrees. In a saucepan, melt butter over medium-high heat. Boil and stir the mushrooms for 5-6 minutes, or until they are tender. When everything is blended, add the flour and 1/8 teaspoon of pepper. Gradually pour in the cream. Cook and stir for approximately 2 minutes, or until the sauce has thickened.

2. In a cup, whisk together the carrot, egg yolk, 2 tsp salt, mushroom sauce, & 1/8 tsp pepper. Crumble the meat over the top and stir well. Unroll the crescent dough and cut it into two rectangles, pressing the holes shut. Place the meatloaf in each rectangle. Bring the sides together and push to seal. If necessary, clean the cracked egg.

3. Place Wellingtons inside an air-fryer pan on an oiled plate in a thin layer. Cook for 18-22 minutes, or until a thermometer inserted into the meatloaf registers 160°F, or until golden brown.

4. Meanwhile, steam the leftover sauce over low heat, then stir in the parsley. Serve the sauce with the Wellingtons.

Nutritional Serving

140 Cal, Protein: 86 g, Carb: 50 g, Fat 25 g

4.19 Air-Fryer Stylish Ravioli

Preparation Time: 20 mins

Cooking Time: 5 mins

Servings: 10

Ingredients

- 1 cup, breadcrumbs
- 1/4 cup, parmesan cheese
- 2 tsp, dried basil
- 1/2 cup, flour
- 2, eggs large
- 1 package, beef ravioli (frozen)
- Cooking spray
- 1 cup, warmed marinara sauce

Steps

1. Preheat the air fryer to 350 degrees. In a small bowl, combine the breadcrumbs, cheese, and basil. Place the flour & eggs in separate shallow bowls. Dip the tortellini in flour to coat both sides and brush off the excess. Dip the shells in the coating, then pat them down with the crumb mix to help them stick.

2. Place the ravioli in a single layer on an oiled tray in air-fryer basket; spray with olive oil in batches. Cook until golden brown, about 3-4 minutes. To cook, flip and spritz with cooking spray. Fry for 3-4 minutes longer, or until lightly browned. If required, top with basil and more Parmesan cheese right away. Serve heated with marinara sauce.

Nutritional Serving

220 Cal, Protein: 110 g, Carb: 80 g, Fat 45 g

4.20 Popcorn Shrimp Tacos with Cabbage Slaw

Preparation Time: 15 mins

Cooking Time: 10 mins

Servings: 8

Ingredients

- 2 cups, coleslaw
- 1/4 cup, cilantro
- 2 tbsp, lime juice
- 2 tbsp, honey
- 1/4 tsp, salt
- 2 large, eggs
- 2 tbsp, milk
- 1/2 cup, flour
- 1-1/2 cup, panko breadcrumbs
- 1 tbsp, ground cumin
- 1 tbsp, garlic powder
- 1 pound, shrimp (non-cooked)
- Cooking spray
- 8, corn tortillas
- 1, medium avocado

Steps

1. In a small bowl, whisk together the cilantro, coleslaw mix, salt, lime juice, pepper, & jalapeño, if desired.

2. Preheat an air fryer to 375 degrees. In a small bowl, whisk together the eggs and milk. In a separate shallow dish, place the flour. In a third small cup, add cumin, Panko, & garlic powder. Dip shrimp in flour to coat both sides and shake off the excess. Dip inside the egg mixture and then pat into the panko mix to assist the coating adhere.

3. In batches, arrange shrimp inside a thin layer in a greased air-fryer bowl and coat with cooking spray. Cook until gently browned, about 2-3 minutes. Turn; spritz with cooking spray. Cook for another 3 minutes, or until the shrimp are pink and gently browned.

4. Serve the shrimp with a coleslaw mixture and avocado tortillas.

Nutritional Serving

140 Cal, Protein: 85 g, Carb: 40 g, Fat 30 g

4.21 Bacon-Wrapped Avocado Wedges

Preparation Time: 20 mins

Cooking Time: 15 mins

Servings: 10

Ingredients

- 2, medium avocados
- 12, bacon strips
- 1/2 cup, mayonnaise
- 2 - 3 tbsp, sriracha chili sauce
- Lime juice 1 - 2 tbsp

Steps

1. Preheat the air fryer to 400 degrees Fahrenheit. Peel and remove the pit from each avocado half. Divide each half into thirds. 1 bacon slice should be wrapped around each avocado wedge. If necessary, work in batches, arranging slices in the thin layer inside the fryer basket & cooking for 10-15 minutes, or until bacon is crispy.

2. In a small bowl, stir together all the sriracha sauce, mayo, lime juice, & zest. Serve the wedges with the sauce on top.

Nutritional Serving

120 Cal, Protein: 75 g, Carb: 30 g, Fat 16 g

4.22 Air-Fryer Steak Fajitas

Preparation Time: 5 mins

Cooking Time: 10 mins

Servings: 8

Ingredients

- 2 large, tomatoes
- 1/2 cup, red onion
- 1/4 cup, lime juice
- 1, pepper jalapeno
- 3 tbsp, cilantro
- 2 tsp, cumin
- 3/4 tsp, salt
- 1, beef flank steak
- 1 large, onion
- 8 inches, whole-wheat tortillas (warmed)

Steps

1. To make the salsa, combine the first 5 ingredients in a small dish with 1 tsp cumin & 1/4 tsp salt. Allow it to rest until ready to serve.

2. Preheat an air fryer to 400 degrees. Season the meat with the remaining cumin and salt. Put the fryer baskets on a plate that has been oiled. Cook for 6-8

minutes on each hand, or until the meat reaches the desired thickness (a thermometer may read 135° for medium-rare, 140° for medium, and 145° for moderate-well). Remove the basket from the oven and set aside for 5 mins to cool.

3. Meanwhile, place the onion in counter-top air-fryer basket. Cook, stirring once or twice, until crisp-tender, about 2-3 minutes. Thin slices the steak against the grain and serve in tortillas with salsa and onion. If desired, garnish with lime & avocado slices.

Nutritional Serving

180 Cal, Protein: 124 g, Carb: 85 g, Fat 25 g

4.23 Air-Fryer Sweet & Sour Pork

Preparation Time: 10 mins

Cooking Time: 5 mins

Servings: 6

Ingredients

- 1/2 cup, pineapple
- 1/2 cup, cider vinegar
- 1/4 cup, sugar
- 1/4 cup, dark brown sugar
- 1/4 cup, ketchup
- 1 tbsp, soy sauce (reduced sodium)
- 1-1/2 tsp, dijon mustard
- 1/2 tsp, garlic powder
- 1, pork tenderloin
- 1/8 tsp, salt
- 1/8 tsp, pepper
- Cooking spray

Steps

1. In a small saucepan, combine the first eight ingredients. Bring it to a boil, then reduce the heat. Cook for 6-8 minutes, occasionally stirring, until the sauce has thickened.

2. Preheat the air fryer to 350 degrees. Season the bacon with salt and pepper. Place the pork on a greased tray inside the air-fryer bowl and spray with cooking mist. Cook until the pork begins to brown all around edges, about 7-8 minutes. Cover the meat with 2 tablespoons of sauce. 11-13 minutes longer, or until a thermometer inserted into the bacon registers at least 145°. Allow 5 minutes for the pork to rest before slicing. Serve with any remaining sauce. If necessary, top with sliced green onions.

Nutritional Serving

190 Cal, Protein: 122 g, Carb: 76 g, Fat 30 g

4.24 Air-Fryer Taco Twists

Preparation Time: 25 mins

Cooking Time: 35 mins

Servings: 9

Ingredients

- 1/3-pound, beef
- 1 large, onion
- 2/3 cup, cheddar cheese
- 1/3 cup, salsa
- 3 tbsp, green chiles (canned & chopped)
- 1/4 tsp, garlic powder
- 1/4 tsp, hot pepper sauce
- 1/8 tsp, salt
- 1/8 tsp, cumin
- 1 tube, freeze crescent rolls

Steps

1. Preheat the air fryer to 300 degrees. In a large pan, cook the beef & onion over medium heat till the meat is just no longer pink, then rinse. Combine sweet pepper sauce, salsa, salt, cheese, garlic powder, & cumin.

2. Unroll crescent roll dough & cut it into four rectangles, pressing the sealing holes together. Place 1/2 cup of the meat mixture in the center of each rectangle. Pinch to cover. Twist and place four corners in the middle. In batches, place in a light coating on (greased) tray in air-fryer bowl. Cook until golden brown, about 18-22 minutes. If desired, serve with seasonings of your choice.

Nutritional Serving

200 Cal, Protein: 100 g, Carb: 60 g, Fat 20 g

4.25 Air-Fryer Potato Chips

Preparation Time: 35 mins

Cooking Time: 15 mins

Servings: 6

Ingredients

- 2, large potatoes
- Olive oil spray
- ½ tsp, sea salt

Steps

1. Preheat air fryer to 360 degrees Fahrenheit. To use a mandolin or a vegetable peeler, finely slice the potatoes. Switch to a large basin and fill it halfway with cold water. Rinse after a 15-minute soak. Soak for another 15 minutes.

2. Drain the potatoes and place them on towels to dry. On the potatoes, spray with cooking spray and season with salt. Place potato slices in batches in a light coating on the greased air-fryer basket plate. Cook for 15-17 minutes, tossing and turning

every 6 minutes, until crisp and gently browned. If desired, garnish with parsley.

Nutritional Serving

140 Cal, Protein: 99 g, Carb: 50 g, Fat 25 g

4.26 Air-Fryer Greek Breadsticks

Preparation Time: 40 mins

Cooking Time: 15 mins

Servings: 6

Ingredients

- 1/4 cup, artichoke hearts (marinated & quartered)
- 2 tbsp, pitted Greek olives
- 1 package, puff pastry (frozen)
- 1 carton, artichoke cream cheese & spreadable spinach
- 2 tbsp, parmesan cheese
- 1 large, egg
- 1 tbsp, water
- 2 tsp, sesame seeds

Steps

1. Preheat an air fryer to 325 degrees. Put the artichokes & olives inside a food processor & process until finely chopped. Unfold one pastry sheet on a floured board and spread half of the mascarpone on halves of the crust. Using a half-artichoke version, comb the artichoke. Half of the Parmesan cheese should be sprinkled on top. Fold the basic half so overfilling & gently press to seal.

2. Replace the cookie, Parmesan cheese, cream cheese, and artichoke combination with remaining cookie, Parmesan cheese, cream cheese, and artichoke mixture. Clean the tips after whisking the water & egg together. Sesame seeds should be sprinkled on top. Each rectangle is divided into 16 3/4-inch-wide strips.

3. On a lubricated tray inside the air-fryer basket, adjust bread slices in a flat piece in batches. Cook for 12-15 minutes, or until golden brown on top.

Nutritional Serving

145 Cal, Protein: 105 g, Carb: 60 g, Fat 12 g

4.27 Air-Fryer Crumb-Topped Sole

Preparation Time: 45 mins

Cooking Time: 15 mins

Servings: 3

Ingredients

- 3 tbsp, mayonnaise
- 3 tbsp, parmesan cheese
- 2 tsp, mustard seed
- 1/4 tsp, Pepper

- 4, sole fillets
- 1 cup, soft breadcrumbs
- 1, onion
- 1/2 tsp, mustard
- 2 tsp, butter
- Cooking spray

Steps

1. Preheat an air fryer to 375 degrees. 2 tablespoons mustard seed, bacon, mayonnaise, & pepper, spread over the tops of the fillets.
2. Place the fish inside a single layer on oiled plate in the air-fryer bowl. Cook for 3-5 minutes, or until the salmon flakes easily with a fork.
3. In a separate bowl, combine breadcrumbs, carrot, ground mustard, and 1 tablespoon remaining cheese; stir in butter. Cook for another 2-3 minutes, or until golden brown. If necessary, top with more green onions.

Nutritional Serving

136 Cal, Protein: 90 g, Carb: 39 g, Fat 17 g

4.28 Air-Fried Radishes

Preparation Time: 21 mins

Cooking Time: 12 mins

Servings: 6

Ingredients

- 2-1/4 pounds, Radishes
- 3 tbsp, Olive oil
- 1 tbsp, Oregano
- 1/4 tsp, Salt
- 1/8 tsp, pepper

Steps

1. Preheat the air fryer to 375°F. Combine all of the ingredients and stir well.
2. In the fryer basin, place radish on a greased tray. Fry for 15 minutes, or until crispy, blending constantly.

Nutritional Serving

122 Cal, Protein: 80 g, Carb: 45 g, Fat 22 g

4.29 Air-Fryer Ham & Egg Pockets

Preparation Time: 10 mins

Cooking Time: 5 mins

Servings: 2

Ingredients

- 1, egg large
- 2 tsp, milk
- 2 tsp, butter
- 1 ounce, deli ham (sliced)
- 2 tbsp, cheddar cheese

- 1 tube, freeze crescent rolls

Steps

1. Preheat the air fryer to 300 degrees. In a small bowl, whisk together the egg and milk. In a small pan, melt the butter until it is sweet. Over medium heat, add the egg mixture and cook & stir till the eggs are formed. Keep your distance from the steam. Combine the cheese & ham in a mixing bowl.

2. Make two rectangles out of the crescent dough. Fold the dough so over contents and press to seal. Place it in a thin layer on an oiled plate in the air-fryer basket. Cook for 8-10 minutes, or till golden brown.

Nutritional Serving

180 Cal, Protein: 110 g, Carb: 88 g, Fat 46 g

4.30 Air-Fryer Eggplant Fries

Preparation Time: 20 mins

Cooking Time: 10 mins

Servings: 6

Ingredients

- 2 large, eggs
- 1/2 cup, parmesan cheese
- 1/2 cup, wheat germ (toasted)
- 1 tsp, Italian seasoning
- 3/4 tsp, garlic salt
- 1, medium eggplant
- Cooking spray
- 1 cup, pasta sauce (meatless)

Steps

1. Preheat an air fryer to 375 degrees. In a small bowl, whisk together the eggs. In a separate small dish, combine the cheese, spices, and wheat germ.

2. Trim the ends of the Eggplant and cut it lengthwise into 1/2-inch thick slices. Split the extended portion into half-inch sections. Cover the Eggplant with the cheese mixture after dipping it in the eggs.

3. Adjust Eggplant in the batches in a single layer on an oiled tray in air-fryer bowl; spray with olive oil. Cook for about 4-5 minutes, or until golden brown. Turn; spritz with cooking spray. Cook for about 4-5 minutes, or until golden brown. Serve immediately with spaghetti sauce.

Nutritional Serving

150 Cal, Protein: 100 g, Carb: 40 g, Fat 22 g

4.31 Air-Fryer Turkey Croquettes

Preparation Time: 15 mins

Cooking Time: 10 mins

Servings: 7

Ingredients

- 2 cups, mashed potatoes
- 1/2 cup, parmesan cheese
- 1/2 cup, Swiss cheese
- 1, shallot
- 2 tsp, rosemary
- 1 tsp, sage
- 1/2 tsp, salt
- 1/4 tsp, Pepper
- 3 cups, cooked turkey
- 1 large, egg
- 2 tbsp, water
- 1-1/4 cup, panko breadcrumbs
- Cooking spray (butter-flavored)

Steps

1. Preheat the air fryer to 350 degrees. In a large mixing bowl, combine the cheese, shallot, salt, pepper, mashed potatoes, sage, & rosemary; stir in the turkey.

2. In a small bowl, whisk together the egg and water. Place the breadcrumbs in a separate shallow cup. To help the coating stick, dip individual croquettes in egg mixture and then pat them into the breadcrumbs.

3. Place the croquettes in a single layer on an oiled tray inside the air-fryer bowl; spray with olive oil. Cook for about 4-5 minutes, or until golden brown. Turn; spritz with cooking spray. Cook until golden brown, about 4-5 minutes. If desired, top with sour cream.

Nutritional Serving

155 Cal, Protein: 21 g, Carb: 17 g, Fat 14 g

4.32 Garlic-Herb Fried Patty Pan Squash

Preparation Time: 10 mins

Cooking Time: 20 mins

Servings: 6

Ingredients

- 5 cups, pattypan squash
- 1 tbsp, olive oil
- 2 cloves, garlic
- 1/2 tsp, salt
- 1/4 tsp, oregano
- 1/4 tsp, thyme (dried)
- 1/4 tsp, Pepper
- 1 tbsp, parsley

Steps

1. Preheat the air fryer to 375°F and place the squash in a mixing dish. Combine the pepper, oil, garlic, salt, oregano, & thyme in a mixing bowl. Toss to evenly coat.

2. Inside the air fryer basin, place squash on a greased tray. Fry for 15 minutes, tossing often, until the vegetables are soft. Parsley is sprayed on top.

Nutritional Serving

147 Cal, Protein: 15 g, Carb: 17 g, Fat 18 g

4.33 Air-Fryer Quinoa Arancini

Preparation Time: 15 mins

Cooking Time: 15 mins

Servings: 12

Ingredients

- 1-3/4 cups, quinoa (cooked)
- 2 large, eggs
- 1 cup, breadcrumbs (seasoned)
- 1/4 cup, parmesan cheese
- 1 tbsp, olive oil
- 2 tbsp, basil
- 1/2 tsp, garlic powder
- 1/2 tsp, salt
- 1/8 tsp, Pepper
- 6 cubes, mozzarella cheese
- Cooking spray

Steps

1. Preheat an air fryer to 375 degrees. Quinoa should be cooked. Combine 1 egg white, 1/2 cup cheese, breadcrumbs, basil oil, and spices in a mixing bowl.
2. Divide into six halves. To completely cover, form each portion into a ball by wrapping it around a cheese ball.
3. Put the remaining egg & 1/2 cup of breadcrumbs in separate shallow cups. Dip quinoa balls in the egg, then roll them in the breadcrumbs. Place on a prepared tray in air-fryer bowl and spray with cooking mist. Cook for about 6-8 minutes, or until golden brown. If necessary, represent with spaghetti sauce

Nutritional Serving

415 Cal, Protein: 15 g, Carb: 14 g, Fat 0 g

4.34 Air-Fryer General Tso's Cauliflower

Preparation Time: 20 mins

Cooking Time: 10 mins

Servings: 2

Ingredients

- 1/2 cup, flour
- 1/2 cup, cornstarch
- 1 tsp, salt
- 1 tsp, baking powder
- 3/4 cup, club soda
- 1, head cauliflower (medium)

Steps

1. Preheat an air fryer to 400 degrees. Combine the baking powder, cornstarch, rice, & salt in a large mixing bowl. Stir in the club soda just before serving. Toss the florets inside the batter and set them on a wire rack to cool. Allow 5 minutes to pass. In the air-fryer basket, put cauliflower in groups on a greased tray. Heat for 10-12 minutes, or until soft and gently browned.

2. Meanwhile, mix together the sauce ingredients, then add the cornstarch and stir until smooth.

3. In a large saucepan, steam canola oil over medium-high heat. Cook and stir in the chilies for 1-2 minutes, or until aromatic. Simmer for 1 minute, or until aromatic, with the garlic, white onions, ginger, & orange zest. Return to saucepan & stir in the orange juice mixture. Bring to a boil; cook and stir for 2-4 minutes until the sauce thickens.

4. Add the cauliflower to the sauce and toss to coat. Represent with rice and finely sliced green onions.

Nutritional Serving

512 Cal, Protein: 15 g, Carb: 6 g, Fat 4 g

4.35 Air-Fryer Pork Chops

Preparation Time: 20 mins

Cooking Time: 10 mins

Servings: 1

Ingredients

- 4 chops, pork loin (boneless)
- 1/3 cup, almond flour
- 1/4 cup, parmesan cheese
- 1 tsp, garlic powder
- 1 tsp, creole seasoning
- 1 tsp, paprika
- Cooking spray

Steps

1. Preheat the Fryer to 375 ° and sprinkle the fryer basket with frying spray. In a small bowl, combine the almond flour, garlic powder, creole spice, cheese, and paprika. Using a variety of flours, coat the pork chops and brush off any excess. Place chops in a single layer inside the air-fryer bowl as required in batches; spritz with nonstick spray

2. Heat until gently browned, 12 to 15 minutes till a 145°F thermometer registers, spritzing and replacing with more cooking spray halfway through. Remove it and keep it damp. Rep with the remaining chops.

Nutritional Serving

117 Cal, Protein: 31 g, Carb: 36 g, Fat 2 g

4.36 Air-Fryer Nacho Hot Dogs

Preparation Time: 15 mins

Cooking Time: 15 mins

Servings: 12

Ingredients

- 6, hot dogs
- 3 sticks, cheddar cheese
- 1-1/4 cups, flour
- 1 cup, Greek yogurt
- 1/4 cup, salsa
- 1/4 tsp, chili powder
- 3 tbsp, jalapeno pepper (chopped & seeded)
- 1 cup, tortilla chips (nacho-flavored)

Steps

1. Cut a slice along each hot dog without cutting it apart; cut a slice including a ½ cheese handle.
2. Preheat the air fryer to 350 degrees. In a large mixing bowl, combine the butter, vinegar, rice, jalapenos, chilli powder, & ½ cup of crumbled tortilla chips to make a smooth mixture. Place the dough on a lightly floured and cut it into sixths. Rolled into 15-inch-long strips and knot one strip with the cheese-stuffed hot dog. Repeat with the remaining dough and hot dogs. Spray the dogs with cooking spray and gently slide them over the broken chips. Spray the fryer containers with cooking spray & place the dogs inside the bowl without touching them, providing room for expansion.
3. Cook for 8-10 minutes in batches, till the dough is lightly toasted and the cheese is melted. If necessary, supplement with more chips, sour cream, and guacamole.

Nutritional Serving

97 Cal, Protein: 5 g, Carb: 23 g, Fat 4 g

4.37 Air-Fryer Raspberry Balsamic Smoked Pork Chops

Preparation Time: 20 mins

Cooking Time: 10 mins

Servings: 14

Ingredients

- 2, large eggs
- 1/4 cup, milk
- 1 cup, panko breadcrumbs
- 1 cup, pecans
- 4 chops, smoked bone-in pork

- 1/4 cup, flour
- Cooking spray
- 1/3 cup, balsamic vinegar
- 2 tbsp, brown sugar
- 2 tbsp, seedless raspberry jam
- 1 tbsp, orange juice (frozen)

Steps

1. Preheat an air fryer to 400 degrees. In a small bowl, whisk together the eggs and milk. In a separate small dish, combine the breadcrumbs and pecans.

2. Flour the pork chops and brush off the excess fat. Dip the shells in the mixture, then pat them into the crumb combination to help them stick. Place chops inside a single layer on an oiled tray on an air-fryer rack in batches; spritz using cooking spray.

3. Heat for 12-15 minutes, or until light brown & a thermometer inserted into the pork registers 145°F, flipping and spritzing halfway through. Meanwhile, combine the other ingredients in a bowl saucepan and bring to the boil. Cook and stir for 6-8 minutes, or until it thickens somewhat. Eat the chops with them.

Nutritional Serving

669 Cal, Protein: 12 g, Carb: 14 g, Fat 2 g

4.38 Air-Fryer Chickpea Fritters with Sweet-Spicy Sauce

Preparation Time: 20 mins

Cooking Time: 15 mins

Servings: 10

Ingredients

- 1 cup, yogurt
- 2 tbsp, sugar
- 1 tbsp, honey
- 1/2 tsp, salt
- 1/2 tsp, Pepper
- 1/2 tsp, red pepper flakes
- 15 ounces, garbanzo beans
- 1 tsp, cumin
- 1/2 tsp, salt
- 1/2 tsp, garlic powder
- 1/2 tsp, ginger
- 1, large egg
- 1/2 tsp, baking soda
- 1/2 cup, cilantro
- 2, onions

Steps

1. Preheat an air fryer to 400 degrees. In a small dish, combine the ingredients and chill until ready to eat.

2. Put spices and chickpeas inside a food processor and pulse until finely ground. Pulse in the baking soda & egg until well mixed. Then, in a separate dish, combine the green onions & cilantro.

3. In batches, drop rounded tablespoons of bean mixture onto the oiled tray in the fryer basket. Fry till golden brown, about 5-6 minutes. Serve with gravy on the side.

Nutritional Serving

213 Cal, Protein: 5 g, Carb: 3 g, Fat 8 g

4.39 Air-Fryer Crispy Sriracha Spring Rolls

Preparation Time: 10 mins

Cooking Time: 10 mins

Servings: 6

Ingredients

- 3 cups, coleslaw
- 3, onions
- 1 tbsp, soy sauce
- 1 tsp, sesame oil
- 1 pound, chicken breasts (boneless & skinless)
- 1 tsp, salt
- 2 packages, cream cheese
- 2 tbsp, sriracha chili sauce
- 24 wrappers, spring roll
- Cooking spray

Steps

1. Preheat the air fryer to 360 degrees. Combine the green onions, coleslaw, soy sauce, & sesame oil in a mixing bowl; set aside whereas the chicken is cooking. Place the chicken inside a single layer on to an oiled plate in an air-fryer bowl. Cook for 18-20 minutes, or until a thermometer inserted in the chicken registers 165 degrees. Remove the chicken and let it cool slightly. Toss the chicken with seasoned salt after finely chopping it.

2. Preheat the air fryer to 400 degrees Fahrenheit. In a large mixing bowl, stir together the cream cheese & Sriracha chilli sauce, then add chicken & coleslaw mixture. With one side of the a spring roll sheet facing you, place roughly 2 tablespoons of filling right below the center of the wrapper. Wet the remaining corners and fold bottom corner overfilling. Overfilling the roll, bend the side corners towards to the center and roll it up firmly, squeezing the tip to seal it.

3. Place spring rolls in a single layer on an oiled tray in air-fryer bowl; spritz with spray bottle in batches. Cook until gently browned, about 5-6 minutes. Turn; spritz with cooking spray. Cook for another 5-6

minutes, or until crisp & golden brown. If desired, top with sweet chilli sauce.

4. 1 inch of undercooked spring rolls should be frozen. Layers are separated with waxed paper & placed in freezer bags. Cook spring rolls according to package directions, adding time as needed.

Nutritional Serving

700 Cal, Protein: 41 g, Carb: 8 g, Fat 0 g

4.40 Air-Fryer Pork Schnitzel

Preparation Time: 30 mins

Cooking Time: 15 mins

Servings: 1

Ingredients

- 1/4 cup, flour
- 1 tsp, salt
- 1/4 tsp, Pepper
- 1, egg large
- 2 tbsp, milk
- 3/4 cup, dry breadcrumbs
- 1 tsp, paprika
- 4, pork sirloin cutlets
- Cooking spray

Steps

1. Preheat an air fryer to 375 degrees. In a small dish, combine the flour, seasoned salt, and pepper. In an another shallow dish, whisk together the egg & milk until well combined. In a third bowl, combine the breadcrumbs and paprika.

2. Using a 1/4-inch beef mallet, pound pork cutlets. Shake off excess flour after dipping the cutlets in flour mixture on both sides. Dip in the shell mixture, then pat in crumb combination to help the coating adhere.

3. Place the pork inside an fryer bowl on to an oiled surface in a single layer; spritz on olive oil. Cook for about 4-5 minutes, or until gently browned. Turn; spritz with cooking spray. Heat for another 4-5 minutes, or until gently browned. Place inside a serving dish and keep warm.

4. Meanwhile, in a small saucepan, whisk together the flour & broth until smooth. Bring to a boil, stirring constantly; cook and stir for 2 minutes, or until thickened. Reduce heat to a minimum. Heat up the dill & sour cream mixture (do not boil). Eat with bacon.

Nutritional Serving

112 Cal, Protein: 5 g, Carb: 10 g, Fat 11 g

4.41 Air-Fryer Green Tomato Stacks

Preparation Time: 20 mins

Cooking Time: 15 mins

Servings: 4

Ingredients

- 1/4 cup, mayonnaise
- 1/4 tsp, lime zest
- 2 tbsp, lime juice
- 1 tsp, thyme
- 1/2 tsp, Pepper
- 1/4 cup, flour
- 2, large egg whites
- 3/4 cup, cornmeal
- 1/4 tsp, salt
- 2, green tomatoes (medium)
- 2, red tomatoes (medium)
- Cooking spray
- 8, Canadian bacon slices

Steps

1. Preheat an air fryer to 375 degrees. Combine the lemon zest, thyme, mayo, juice, & 1/4 teaspoon pepper in a mixing bowl; chill until ready to serve. Put the flour in one shallow basin and the egg whites in another shallow one. In a third dish, combine the cornmeal, salt, & the remaining 1/4 teaspoon of pepper.

2. Each tomato should be cut into four crosswise slices. Apply a small layer of flour to each slice and shake off the excess. Dip inside egg whites, then in the cornmeal mixture.

3. Spritz with olive oil and put tomatoes in batches inside an air-fryer pan on a prepared tray. Cook until it's gently browned, about 4-6 minutes. Turn; spritz with cooking spray. Cook for another 4-6 minutes, or until golden brown.

4. For each meal, stack 1 slice of bacon, green tomato, & red tomato. Make a statement with the gravy.

Nutritional Serving

85 Cal, Protein: 12 g, Carb: 14 g, Fat 3 g

4.42 Air-Fryer Pretzel-Crusted Catfish

Preparation Time: 25 mins

Cooking Time: 10 mins

Servings: 3

Ingredients

- 6 oz, catfish fillets
- 1/2 tsp, salt
- 1/2 tsp, Pepper

- 2, eggs large
- 1/3 cup, Dijon mustard
- 2 tbsp, 2% milk
- 1/2 cup, flour
- 4 cups, honey mustard pretzels (small)
- Cooking spray

Steps

1. Preheat an air fryer to 325 degrees. Season the catfish with salt and pepper. Whisk together the mustard, eggs, & milk in a small bowl. Put flour and pretzels in separate shallow basins. Cover all flour fillets with a layer of flour, then pour in the egg mixture and top with pretzels.

2. Spray the fillets with olive oil & arrange them in a thin layer just on oiled tray inside the fryer basket in batches. Cook for 10-12 minutes, or until the salmon flakes easily with a fork. If necessary, use lemon slices to represent.

Nutritional Serving

369 Cal, Protein: 36 g, Carb: 14 g, Fat 12 g

4.43 Air-Fryer French Toast Cups with Raspberries

Preparation Time: 15 mins

Cooking Time: 15 mins

Servings: 9

Ingredients

- 2 slices, Italian bread
- 1/2 cup, raspberries
- 2 ounces, cream cheese
- 2, large eggs
- 1/2 cup, milk
- 1 tbsp, maple syrup

Steps

1. Half of the bread cubes should be divided into two 8-ounce oiled cubes. Custard in cups. To sprinkle, use raspberries and cream cheese. Cover with the rest of the spaghetti. In a separate dish, whisk together the sugar, eggs, & syrup, sprinkle over the bread. Cover and chill for at least an hour.

2. Preheat an air fryer to 325 degrees. Place custard cups on a platter in an air-fryer basket. Preheat oven to 350°F and bake for 12-15 minutes, or until golden brown & fluffy.

3. Meanwhile, in a small saucepan, whisk together cornstarch and water until smooth. Combine 1-1/2 cups raspberries, lemon zest, lime juice, and syrup in a mixing bowl. Bring it to a boil, then reduce the heat. Cook and stir for about 2 minutes, or until the sauce has thickened.

Cool slightly after straining and extracting the seeds.

4. Gently fold in the leftover 1/2 cup fresh berries into to the syrup. If preferred, sprinkle cinnamon on the French toast pieces & serve with syrup.

Nutritional Serving

512 Cal, Protein: 12 g, Carb: 8 g, Fat 0 g

4.44 Air Fryer Ham & Cheese Turnovers

Preparation Time: 10 mins

Cooking Time: 15 mins

Servings: 5

Ingredients

- 1 tube, freeze pizza crust
- 1/4-pound, black forest deli ham
- 1 medium, pear
- 1/4 cup, walnuts
- 2 tbsp, blue cheese

Steps

1. Preheat an air fryer to 400 degrees. On a lightly floured board, unroll the pizza foundation into a 12-inch length. Make four triangles out of the dough. Diagonally within 1/2-inch, layer pork, half pear pieces, walnuts, and blue cheese on half of each square. From the periphery. Fold one corner to the other side to form a triangle so over filling; use a fork to seal the edges.

2. Turnovers should be adjusted in batches and placed in a single layer on a greased tray inside the air-fryer bowl, spritzed with such a cooking mist. Heat for 4-6 minutes on each side until lightly browned. Finish with the remaining pear slices as a garnish.

Nutritional Serving

212 Cal, Protein: 4 g, Carb: 1.6 g, Fat 8 g

4.45 Air-Fryer Shrimp Po'boys

Preparation Time: 20 mins

Cooking Time: 10 mins

Servings: 3

Ingredients

- 1/2 cup, mayonnaise
- 1 tbsp, creole mustard
- Cornichons 1 tbsp
- Shallot 1 tbsp
- 1-1/2 tsp, lemon juice
- 1/8 tsp, cayenne pepper

Steps

1. In a shallow bowl, combine the ingredients. Keep refrigerated in an airtight container until ready to use.

2. Preheat an air fryer to 375 degrees. In a small plate, combine the pepper, garlic powder, salt, rice, & cayenne. In a small shallow bowl, whisk together the egg, milk, & spicy pepper sauce. Place the coconut in a separate shallow basin. Toss the shrimp into flour to coat both sides and shake off the excess. Dip inside the egg mix, then put the coconut on top to keep it in place.

3. Arrange the shrimps in a single layer on an oiled tray in air-fryer bowl spritz with olive oil. Cook for 3-4 mins on each side, or until the shrimp becomes golden and the coconut is lightly toasted.

4. Spread remoulade on the cut side of the buns. On top, arrange the shrimp, lettuce, and tomato.

Nutritional Serving

512 Cal, Protein: 2 g, Carb: 6 g, Fat 8 g

4.46 Air-Fryer Papas Rellenas

Preparation Time: 20 mins

Cooking Time: 15 mins

Servings: 8

Ingredients

- 2-1/2 pounds, potatoes
- 1-pound, lean ground beef
- 1 small, green Pepper
- 1 small, onion
- 1/2 cup, tomato sauce
- 1/2 cup, green olives with pimientos
- 1/2 cup, raisins
- 1-1/4 tsp, salt
- 1-1/4 tsp, Pepper
- 1/2 tsp, paprika
- 1 tsp, garlic powder
- 2, large eggs
- 1 cup, breadcrumbs (seasoned)
- Cooking spray

Steps

1. In a big saucepan, place the potatoes & cover them with water. Just bring it to a low heat. Reduce heat to low, cover, and cook for 15-20 minutes, or until vegetables are soft. Meanwhile, in a large pan, sauté the green pepper, beef, and onion over medium heat till the meat is just no longer pink, then rinse. Combine the olives, pasta sauce, raisins, 1/4 tsp cinnamon, 1/4 teaspoon pepper, and paprika in a mixing bowl.

2. Drain the potatoes and mash them with the garlic powder and the remaining 1 tsp of salt and pepper. Form two tbsp of potato into a patty with a tbsp of stuffing in the center. Make a ball out of the

potatoes by wrapping them around the filling. All you have to do is repeat.

3. Separate the eggs and breadcrumbs into shallow basins. Dip the potatoes balls in the eggs, then coat the roll with breadcrumbs. Preheat the oven to 400 degrees Fahrenheit. Sprinkle with spray bottle and place into batches in a fryer bowl onto an oiled tray. Cook for 14-16 minutes, or until brown is transparent.

Nutritional Serving

412 Cal, Protein: 2 g, Carb: 12 g, Fat 8 g

4.47 Air-Fryer Herb & Cheese-Stuffed Burgers

Preparation Time: 20 mins

Cooking Time: 15 mins

Servings: 4

Ingredients

- 2, green onions
- 2 tbsp, parsley
- 4 tsp, Dijon mustard
- 3 tbsp, breadcrumbs
- 2 tbsp, ketchup
- 1/2 tsp, salt
- 1/2 tsp, rosemary
- 1/4 tsp, sage leaves
- 1-pound, lean ground beef
- 2 ounces, cheddar cheese
- 4, hamburger buns

Steps

1. Preheat an air fryer to 375 degrees. In a small bowl, combine chopped parsley, green onions, & 2 tbsp mustard. In a separate cup, combine the ketchup, crumbs, spices, & the remaining 2 tablespoons of mustard. Add the steak to bread crumb mixture & stir gently but thoroughly.

2. Form the ingredients into 8 thin patties. Put the cheese (sliced) in the center of four patties and top with the green onion mixture. Cover with remaining patties, pressing the sides together firmly and thoroughly.

3. Place the burgers in a light coating just on tray inside the air-fryer bowl in batches. Cooking time is eight minutes. Cook for another 9 minutes, or until a thermometer placed into the burger registers 160 degrees. Serve burgers on buns, with additional toppings as desired.

Nutritional Serving

369 Cal, Protein: 29 g, Carb: 29 g, Fat 14 g

4.48 Nashville Hot Special Chicken

Preparation Time: 30 mins

Cooking Time: 10 mins

Servings: 6

Ingredients

- 2 tbsp, pickle juice
- Hot pepper sauce, 2 tbsp
- 1 tsp, salt
- 2 pounds, chicken tenderloins
- 1 cup, flour
- 1/2 tsp, Pepper
- 1 large, egg
- 1/2 cup, Buttermilk
- Cooking spray
- 1/2 cup, olive oil
- 2 tbsp, cayenne Pepper
- 2 tbsp, dark brown sugar
- 1 tsp, paprika
- 1 tsp, chili powder
- 1/2 tsp, garlic powder
- Pickle slices

Steps

1. In a cup and shallow bath, combine 1 tbsp pickle juice, 1 tbsp hot sauce, and 1/2 teaspoon salt. Switch your coat over once you've connected the bird. Freeze for 1 hour in an airtight container. Drain, reserving part of the marinade.

2. Preheat an air fryer to 375 degrees. In a small bowl, combine the starch, the other 1/2 tsp salt, and the pepper. In a separate small cup, combine bacon, Buttermilk, 1 tbsp pickle juice, and 1 tablespoon spicy sauce. Dip chicken in flour to coat both sides and shake off the excess. Dip into the egg mixture, and back into the flour mixture.

3. Spritz the chicken with cooking spray & arrange it in a single layer on the well tray in air-fryer bowl. Cook for a total of 5-6 minutes, or until golden brown. Turn; spritz with cooking spray. Cook for another 5-6 minutes, or until golden brown.

4. Combine milk, smoked paprika, brown sugar, spices, and heated chicken in a large mixing bowl. Cover with the lid. Eat with pickles.

Nutritional Serving

413 Cal, Protein: 29 g, Carb: 20 g, Fat 21 g

4.49 Air-Fryer Salmon with Maple-Dijon Glaze

Preparation Time: 10 mins

Cooking Time: 15 mins

Servings: 4

Ingredients

- 3 tbsp, butter
- 3 tbsp, maple syrup
- 1 tbsp, Dijon mustard
- 1, lemon medium
- 1, garlic clove
- 1 tbsp, olive oil
- 1/4 tsp, salt
- 1/4 tsp, Pepper
- 4 ounces, salmon fillets

Steps

1. Preheat an air fryer to 400 degrees Fahrenheit.
2. In a deep saucepan, melt the butter over medium and high heat. Toss in the mustard, maple syrup, lemon juice, & garlic, minced. Reduce the heat to low and continue to cook for another 2-3 minutes, or until the mixture has thickened noticeably.
3. Drizzle olive oil over the fish and season with salt & pepper. Place the fish on a single sheet inside an air fryer basin. Cook for 5-7 minutes, or until the fish is lightly browned and flaking easily with a fork. Drizzle with sauce shortly before serving.

Nutritional Serving

339 Cal, Protein: 19 g, Carb: 11 g, Fat 23 g

4.50 Air Fryer Tortellini with Prosciutto

Preparation Time: 25 mins

Cooking Time: 10 mins

Servings: 24

Ingredients

- 1 tbsp, olive oil
- 3 tbsp, onion
- 4 cloves, garlic
- 15 ounces, tomato puree
- 1 tbsp, basil
- 1/4 tsp, salt
- 1/4 tsp, pepper

Steps

1. In a small saucepan, heat the oil over medium-high heat. Cook and stir in the garlic & onion for 3-4 mins, or until tender. Stir in the basil, tomato puree, salt, & pepper. Bring it to a boil, then reduce the heat. Cook for 10 minutes before opening. Only remain drenched.
2. Meanwhile, prepare the air fryer to 350°F. In a small cup, whisk together the eggs and milk. In a separate dish,

combine parsley, garlic powder, crumbs, cheese, & salt.

3. Toss the tortellini in the egg mixture, then coat it with the bread crumb mixture. Toss tortellini with olive oil and arrange inside a thin layer inside an fryer basket on a prepared tray. Cook for about 4-5 minutes, or until golden brown. Turn; spritz with cooking spray. Heat for another 4-5 minutes, or until gently browned. Serve with a dollop of sauce and a sprinkling of fresh basil, minced.

Nutritional Serving

38 Cal, Protein: 1 g, Carb: 5 g, Fat 1 g

4.51 Air-Fryer Cumin Carrots

Preparation Time: 20 mins

Cooking Time: 15 mins

Servings: 4

Ingredients

- 2 tsp, coriander seeds
- 2 tsp, cumin seeds
- 1 pound, carrots
- 1 tbsp, coconut oil
- 2 cloves, garlic
- 1/4 tsp, salt
- 1/8 tsp, pepper

Steps

1. Preheat an air fryer to 325 degrees. In a small dry pan over medium heat, toast the coriander & cumin seeds for 50-60 seconds, or until fragrant, turning often. Use a spice grinder or a mortar and pestle until finely ground.

2. In a large mixing basin, place the carrots. Swirl to coat with melted onion, coconut oil, salt, melted garlic, & pepper. Put the fryer bowl on a plate that has been greased.

3. Cook for 12-15 minutes, tossing often, until crispy and golden brown. If necessary, top with cilantro.

Nutritional Serving

186 Cal, Protein: 1 g, Carb: 12 g, Fat 4 g

4.52 Air-Fryer Mini Chimichangas

Preparation Time: 60 mins

Cooking Time: 10 mins

Servings: 14

Ingredients

- 1 pound, beef
- 1, medium onion
- 1 envelope, taco seasoning
- 3/4 cup, water

- 3 cups, Monterey jack cheese
- 1 cup, sour cream
- 4 ounces, green chiles
- 14, eggs roll wrappers
- 1 large, egg white
- Cooking spray
- Salsa

Steps

1. In a large pan, cook the beef & onion over medium heat till the meat is just no longer pink, then wash. Combine the water & taco seasoning in a mixing bowl. Just bring it to a low heat. Reduce heat to low and cook for 5 minutes with the lid open, stirring occasionally. Remove from the heat and set aside to cool somewhat.

2. Preheat an air fryer to 375 degrees. In a large cup, mix sour cream, cheese, & chilies. Mix in the meat mixture. Place one egg roll wrapper on work area with one tip facing you. Fill the middle of the cup with 1/3 of the contents. Fold one-third of your wrapper's bottom over the filling and fold sideways

3. Brush the top tip with egg white and wrap it up to secure it. Rep with the remaining filling and wrappers.

4. Chimichangas should be placed in batches on an oiled tray in air-fryer bowl and spritzed with olive oil. Heat for 3-4 minutes on each side until lightly browned. Serve immediately with salsa and additional sour cream.

Nutritional Serving

294 Cal, Protein: 16 g, Carb: 23 g, Fat 15 g

4.53 Air-Fryer Fiesta Chicken Fingers

Preparation Time: 20 mins

Cooking Time: 15 mins

Servings: 4

Ingredients

- 3/4-pound, boneless skinless chicken breasts
- 1/2 cup, Buttermilk
- 1/4 tsp, Pepper
- 1 cup, flour
- 3 cups, corn chips
- 1 envelope, taco seasoning
- Salsa

Steps

1. Preheat an air fryer to 400 degrees. Using a 1/2-inch meat mallet, pound the chicken breasts. 1-inch-thick slices Strips are rather large.

2. In a small bowl, combine the Buttermilk and Pepper. In a separate shallow dish,

place the flour. Combine corn chips & taco seasoning in the 3rd bowl. Drop chicken in flour to cover both sides & shake off the excess. To help the corn muffin mixture stick to the coating, dip it in the buttermilk mixture, and then pat it in.

3. Put the chicken in a single layer onto a greased tray inside the air-fryer bowl, spritzed with olive oil. Cook for 7-8 mins on each side until the chicken isn't any longer pink and the coating is gently browned. Rep with the remaining chicken. Serve with the ranch's dip or salsa.

Nutritional Serving

676 Cal, Protein: 24 g, Carb: 60 g, Fat 36 g

4.54 Air-Fryer Everything Bagel Chicken Strips

Preparation Time: 10 mins

Cooking Time: 15 mins

Servings: 4

Ingredients

- 1, bagel (day-old)
- 1/2 cup, panko breadcrumbs
- 1/2 cup, parmesan cheese
- 1/4 tsp, red pepper flakes
- 1/4 cup, butter
- 1 pound, chicken tenderloins
- 1/2 tsp, salt

Steps

1. Preheat an air fryer to 400 degrees. Process the broken bagel in a food processor until coarse crumbs form. Toss ½ cup bagel crumbs with panko, pepper seasoning, & cheese in a small basin.

2. Inside a microwave-safe small dish, reheat melted butter. Season the chicken with salt. Dip in warm butter to help bind, then cover in crumb mixture and press down. In batches, place the chicken on a greased tray inside the air-fryer bowl in a thin layer.

3. Cook for 7 mins, then flip the chicken. Cook for another 7-8 minutes, or until the chicken isn't any longer pink and the coating is gently browned.

Nutritional Serving

269 Cal, Protein: 31 g, Carb: 8 g, Fat 13 g

4.55 Air-Fryer Peach-Bourbon Wings

Preparation Time: 35 mins

Cooking Time: 15 mins

Servings: 12

Ingredients

- 1/2 cup, preserve peaches
- 2 tbsp, bourbon

- 1 tbsp, brown sugar
- 1/4 tsp, salt
- 2 tbsp, white vinegar
- 1, garlic cloves
- 1 tsp, cornstarch
- 1-1/2 tsp, water
- 2 pounds, chicken wings

Steps

1. Preheat an air fryer to 400 degrees. Blend the jellies, brown garlic, sugar, & salt in a food processor until smooth. Place it in a small casserole dish. Remove the bourbon and vinegar and heat the mixture. Reduce heat to low and cook, uncovered, for 4-6 mins, or until the sauce has softly thickened.

2. In a separate bowl, whisk together the cornstarch & water until smooth, then add the preserves mixture. Return to the a boil, stirring constantly, for 1-2 minutes, or until the sauce has thickened. Save ¼ cup sauce for serving.

3. With a sharp knife, cut through the two joints on every chicken wing; cut the tips of the wings. In batches, arrange wing portions inside a single layer on to an oiled tray inside the air-fryer bowl. Cook for 6 mins, then flip and spritz with a preserves mixture. Cooked for a further 6-8 minutes before browning and letting the juices flow free. Serve the wings right away with the sauce you set out.

Nutritional Serving

79 Cal, Protein: 5 g, Carb: 7 g, Fat 3 g

4.56 Turkey Breast Tenderloins in the Air Fryer

Preparation Time: 5 mins

Cooking Time: 25 mins

Servings: 6

Ingredients

- 1 tsp, dill weed
- 1 tsp, dried thyme
- 1 tsp, oregano dried
- ¾ tsp, salt
- 1 tsp, onion sliced
- ¼ cup, butter
- ¼ tsp, Pepper
- 3 cups, carrots
- 4, celery ribs
- 1 tbsp, olive oil
- 2 medium, onions
- ¼ cup, water
- 2 tsp, cornstarch
- 8, turkey breast tenderloins

Steps

1. Preheat the oven to 425 degrees Fahrenheit. In a small dish, combine the first six ingredients. Toss the veggies with 2 tablespoons of the spice mixture and the butter. Place on a plate to roast. Cover and bake for 15 minutes.

2. In the meanwhile, brush the remaining spice mixture over the turkey. Place the veggies on the edges of the pan and the turkey in the middle. Cook for 20-25 minutes, uncovered, or until a thermometer put into the turkey registers, 165°F, and the veggies are tender.

3. Save half of the turkey for Buffalo Turkey Linguine or another usage. Remove the remaining turkey & veggies to a serving plate and keep warm.

4. Pour the cooking liquids into a small saucepan. Stir together the cornstarch & water until smooth, then gradually pour into the pan. Cook and stir for 2 minutes, or until the sauce has thickened. Serve with turkey and carrots.

Nutritional Serving

168 Cal, Protein: 34 g, Carb: 0 g, Fat 2 g

4.57 Air Fryer Rotisserie Roasted Whole Chicken

Preparation Time: 60 mins

Cooking Time: 10 mins

Servings: 6

Ingredients

- 5 pounds, whole chicken
- ½, lemon
- ¼ whole, onion
- 4 springs, thyme
- 4 springs, rosemary
- Olive oil spray
- 1 tsp, thyme ground
- 1 tsp, onion powder
- 1 tsp, garlic powder
- Salt n pepper to taste

Steps

1. Cut the extra fat from around the bird, generally around the neck & tail portion.
2. Dry the chicken with a paper towel.
3. Season with salt & pepper and drizzle with olive oil.
4. Remove chicken from of the air fryer to allow it to rest before slicing.

Nutritional Serving

166 Cal, Protein: 24 g, Carb: 1 g, Fat 6 g

Chapter 5: Dinner Recipes

5.1 Air Fryer Shrimp

Preparation Time: 15 mins

Cooking Time: 24 mins

Servings: 4

Ingredients

- 1 lb, Shrimp (if necessary, separate the tail and shell)
- 1 ½ tsp, Olive oil
- 1 ½ tsp, Lemon juice
- 1 ½ tsp, Honey
- 2 pieces, Minced garlic
- 1/8 tsp, Salt

For garnishing

- Cilantro
- Wedge Sliced lime wedges

Steps

1. In a large mixing bowl, mix all of the ingredients, including lime juice, garlic, olive oil, honey, & salt.
2. Add the shrimp & mix for 25-30 minutes.
3. Preheat an air fryer to 395 degrees Fahrenheit/200 degrees Celsius.
4. Shake off any remaining sauces on the shrimp and set the whole sampling in air fryer.
5. Gently shake the basket and cook over moderate heat before transferring to air fryer. Cook for 3-4 minutes longer, or until the shrimp is pink and fully cooked.
6. Serve with lime slices & cilantro on the side.

Nutritional Serving

415 Cal, Protein: 23 g, Carb: 32 g, Fat 23 g

5.2 Air Fryer Loaded Pork Burritos

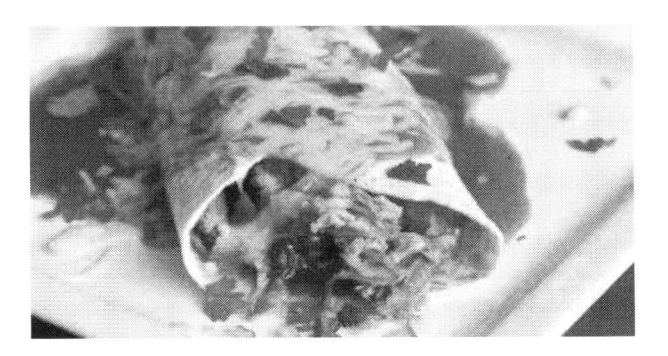

Preparation Time: 35 mins

Cooking Time: 10 mins

Servings: 6

Ingredients

- ¾ cup, Thawed limeade concentrate
- 1 tbsp, Olive oil
- 2 tsp, Salt
- 1 1/2 tsp, Pepper
- 1-1/2 lbs, Boneless pork loin cut into thin slices
- 1 cup, Seeded fresh diced tomatoes
- 1 small, diced Green pepper
- 1 small, Chopped onion
- 1/4 cup, Fresh cilantro chopped
- 1 small, jalapeno pepper diced and seeded
- 1 tsp, lime juice
- 1/4 tsp, Garlic powder
- 1 cup, long-grain of uncooked rice
- 3 cups, Monterey Jack shredded cheese
- 6 (12 inches), flour tortillas
- 1 can (15 ounces), black beans cleaned and drained
- 1-1/2 cups, Whipped cream
- Cooking mist

Steps

1. In a large shallow dish, combine the oil, salt, limeade, and pepper; add the pork. Cover and chill for at least twenty minutes after turning to coat.
2. In a shallow dish, combine the peppers, onion, green pepper, lime juice, cilantro, jalapeño, garlic powder, and remaining salt and black pepper for the salsa.
3. Cook the rice according to the package directions. Combine the remaining coriander in a bowl.
4. Removed the meat from the marinade and rinsed it. Preheat the fryer to 355°F. Sprinkle the pork with cooking mist and cook in batches on the greased tray in air-fryer basket. Cook for 8-ten min, or until the pork isn't any longer pink, flipping halfway through.
5. 1/3 cup cheese should be sprinkled on each tortilla. Cover each with pork, salsa, rice mix, black beans, & sour cream. Bend the sides, and the filling will come to a stop. Serve with the salsa that was leftover.

Nutritional Serving

910 Cal, Protein: 50 g, Carb: 82 g, Fat 24 g

5.3 Air Fryer Sweet & Sour Pineapple Pork

Preparation Time: 25 mins

Cooking Time: 20 mins

Servings: 4

Ingredients

- 8 ounces or 1 can, Smashed unsweetened smashed pineapple
- 1 cup, Vinegar
- ½ cup, Sugar
- ½ cup, dark brown Sugar packed
- ½ cup, Ketchup
- 2 cups, Soy sauce
- 1 tbsp, Mustard Dijon
- 1 tsp, Garlic
- 2 ¾ lb, pork tenderloins
- ¼ tsp, Salt
- ¼ tsp, Pepper
- Diced onions

Steps

1. In a large frying pan, bring together the first eight ingredients and cook over low heat. Stir it often and let it out for 15-20 minutes till it thickens.
2. Preheat air fryer to 350 degrees Fahrenheit. Season the pork with salt and pepper. Place the pork on an oiled plate in an air-fryer bowl. Cook until the pork begins to brown all around edges, about 7-8 minutes. Combine the sauce with the top of pork. Cook for 8-10 minutes, or until the temperature reaches 146° C. Allow the pork to rest for 5 minutes before slicing. Serve with spicy sauce on the side. If desired, garnish with chopped green onions.

Nutritional Serving

489 Cal, Protein: 35 g, Carb: 71 g, Fat 6 g

5.4 Air Fryer Green Tomato BLT

Preparation Time: 20 mins

Cooking Time: 10 mins

Servings: 4

Ingredients

- 10 ounces, green tomatoes
- ½ tsp, salt
- ¼ tsp, pepper
- 1, beaten large egg

- ¼ cup, flour
- 1 cup, panko bread crumbs
- Cooking mist
- ½ cup, mayonnaise
- 2, green onions diced
- 1 tsp, freshly cut dill
- 8 slices, wheat bread
- 8 strips, cooked pork
- 4 leaves, lettuce chopped

Steps

1. Preheat air fryer to 350 degrees Fahrenheit. Each tomato was cut into four pieces crosswise. The seasonings of salt and black pepper were applied. Egg, flour, & breadcrumbs were placed in a separate shallow container. Toss the tomato chunks in flour, brush out the excess, and then dip them into the egg, then the bread crumbs mixture.
2. Organize tomato slices in the single layer on the oiled tray in air-fryer basket & spray with cooking spray in batches. Heat until golden brown, about 5-6 minutes.
3. In a separate bowl, combine the mayonnaise, dill, & green onions. Place 2 strips of bacon, 1 lettuce leaf, and 2 tomato slices on each of 4 bread slices. Spread the mayonnaise mixture over the remaining bread pieces and serve.

Nutritional Serving

390 Cal, Protein: 16 g, Carb: 45 g, Fat 17 g

5.5 Air fryer roasted green beans

Preparation Time: 40 mins

Cooking Time: 25 mins

Servings: 4

Ingredients

- 1 lb, green beans fresh
- ½ pound, mushrooms
- 1 small, onion, finely chopped
- 2 tsp, olive oil
- 1 tsp, italian seasoning
- ¼ tsp, salt
- 1/8 tsp, mustard

Steps

1. Preheat a air fryer to 375 degrees Fahrenheit. In a large mixing basin, combine all of the ingredients.
2. Arrange veggies on a greased plate in air-fryer buckets. Cook for ten to twelve minutes, or up until the vegetables are just

tender. Cook for a further 10-12 minutes on the other side until browned.

Nutritional Serving

60 Cal, Protein: 1 g, Carb: 6 g, Fat 3 g

5.6 Air fryer spicy chicken breasts

Preparation Time: 15 mins

Cooking Time: 15 mins

Servings: 6

Ingredients

- 2 cups, buttermilk
- 2 tsp, salt
- 2 cups, breadcrumbs
- 2 tbsp, mustard dijon
- 2 tsp, pepper sauce hot
- 1 or 1/2 tsp, garlic powder
- 1 cup, corn flour
- 8 ounces, breast pieces of chicken
- 2 tsp, canola oil
- 1/2 teaspoon, poultry seasoning
- 1/2 tsp, mustard
- 1/2 tsp, paprika
- 1/2 tsp, cayenne pepper
- 1/4 tsp, oregano
- 1/4 tsp, dry parsley flakes

Steps

1. Preheat the air fryer to 375 degrees Celsius. In a large mixing bowl, combine the first five ingredients. Change the coat after mixing with the chicken. Refrigerate for at least sixty minutes or overnight if sealed.

2. Remove the sauces from chicken and discard them. Mix the remaining ingredients in a large mixing basin and stir to combine. Using the brush, marinate the chicken in the marinade. Place it in a thin layer on greased plate in the air-fryer basket. Cook for approximately 25 minutes, or until the thermometer reads 170 degrees, turning halfway through. Return all of the chicken to air fryer & cook for another 3-4 minutes, or until cooked through.

Nutritional Serving

450 Cal, Protein: 36 g, Carb: 42 g, Fat 17 g

5.7 Air fryer Reuben Calzones

Preparation Time: 15 mins

Cooking Time: 10 mins

Servings: 4

Ingredients

- 13.8 ounces, pizza crust refrigerated
- 4 pieces, Swiss cheese

- 1 cup, Sauerkraut
- ½ lb, corned beef cooked
- Thousand Island salad dressing

Steps

1. Preheat the air fryer to four hundred degrees Fahrenheit. Unroll the pizza dough and flatten into 14-inch squares on a lightly floured surface. Cut into four blocks. Within 1/2 inch of the sides, layer 1 horizontally over halfway of each piece of cheese & a fourth of bratwurst and corned beef. Fold one corner to the other corner to form a triangle over filling; use a fork to seal the edges. Place two calzones in air-fryer basket in the thin layer on greased plate.
2. Cook for ten to twelve minutes, flipping halfway through, until golden brown. Serve with the salad and sauce.

Nutritional Serving

430 Cal, Protein: 21 g, Carb: 49 g, Fat 17 g

5.8 Teriyaki Salmon Fillets with Broccoli

Preparation Time: 20 mins

Cooking Time: 10 mins

Servings: 5

Ingredients

- 2 cups, Small cloves of broccoli
- 2 tsp, Vegetable oil
- As needed, black pepper and salt
- 1 tbsp, Soy sauce
- 1 tsp, Sugar
- 1 tsp, Vinegar
- 1/4 teaspoon, Cornstarch
- 1 1/2-inch, Diced ginger
- 2 6 ounces, salmon fillets
- 1 slice, Scallion
- Cooked white rice for serving

Steps

1. Toss the broccoli with 1 tsp of oil in a mixing basin. Season to taste with salt and pepper. Shift the broccoli in a 3.5-quart air fryer.
2. Combine the sugar, vinegar, soy sauce, cornstarch, and ginger in a small bowl. Spray the remaining 1 tablespoon of oil on both sides of the salmon fillets, then top with the sauce. Arrange the salmon skin-side down on top of broccoli.
3. Bake at 390 degrees F for 8 to 10 minutes, average thickness of the fillets, until the broccoli is soft and the salmon is cooked through. Transfer to serving dishes and top with scallion pieces and rice.

Nutritional Serving

568 Cal, Protein: 37 g, Carb: 57 g, Fat 20 g

5.9 Air fryer steak with garlic herb butter

Preparation Time: 15 mins

Cooking Time: 20 mins

Servings: 2

Ingredients

- 1 lb, sirloin steak
- Black pepper n salt
- 4 tsp, Butter
- 1 tsp, thinly sliced parsley
- 1 tbsp, Chives
- 1 clove, Garlic
- 1 tbsp, crushed red pepper flakes

Steps

1. Permit the steak to sit overnight for 35 minutes before baking.
2. Preheat the 3.5-quart air fryer to 405 degrees F. On both sides, sprinkle the steak with something like a big pinch of salt & a couple of heaps of black pepper. Place the steak pieces in air fryer bowl in the center and cook until done, about 12 minutes for medium-rare. Move the steak to a chopping board and let aside for 10 minutes.
3. Meanwhile, combine the parsley, chives, butter, garlic, and smashed red pepper in a small mixing dish. Cut the meat against the grain into 14-inch chunks. Toss the top with the garlic-herb butter.

Nutritional Serving

774 Cal, Protein: 47 g, Carb: 1 g, Fat 64 g

5.10 Air fryer fried rice with sesame sriracha sauce

Preparation Time: 15 mins

Cooking Time: 16 mins

Servings: 2

Ingredients

- 2 cups, White cooked rice
- 1 tbsp., Oil
- 2 tsp, Sesame oil toasted
- Salt and black pepper
- 1 tsp, Sriracha
- 1 tsp, Soya sauce
- 1/2 tsp, Sesame seeds
- 1, Big egg
- 1 cup, Peas & carrots

Steps

1. Combine the vegetable oil, rice, sesame oil, and one tablespoon of water in a cup. Season with salt & pepper to taste, then stir the rice to completely coat it. For a 7-inch round air fryer, use a metal cake pan or foil Pan instead.

2. Place the Pan inside a 5.3-quart fryer & cook at 350 degrees F for roughly 14 minutes, stirring halfway through, until the rice is gently cooked and crispy.
3. Meanwhile, combine the sesame seeds, sriracha, & soy sauce, and 1 teaspoon sesame oil in a shallow cup.
4. Cook for a further 4 minutes, covered, until egg is cooked through. To distribute the potato, reopen the bag and add the peas & carrots to the rice. Close the lids and simmer for another 2 minutes to warm the peas and carrots.
5. Drizzle some of sauce on top and serve.

Nutritional Serving

392 Cal, Protein: 11 g, Carb: 54 g, Fat 14 g

5.11 Air fryer Roast Chicken

Preparation Time: 15 mins

Cooking Time: 90 mins

Servings: 6

Ingredients

- Cooking spray (nonstick)
- 3 - 3 1/2 pounds, chicken
- 1 tbsp, olive oil
- Black pepper and salt
- New rosemary
- 8-12 cloves, garlic
- ½ tsp, lemon

Steps

1. Preheat the frying Pan to 375 degrees Fahrenheit and coat the dish with nonstick cooking spray.
2. Add the olive oil to soften the chicken's exterior.
3. The interior and exterior of the bird is sprayed with 1 tsp of salt and a number of peppercorns. Utilize garlic, spices, and lemon juice to fill the void. Place the chicken breast-side up in the bowl, pressing it down so that it does not touch the fryer's top.
4. Cook the chicken there in thick portion of the thigh at 160 degrees for 65 minutes, or until golden and crisp.

Nutritional Serving

444 Cal, Protein: 31 g, Carb: 3 g, Fat 28 g

5.12 Air Fryer Mini Swedish Meatballs

Preparation Time: 20 mins

Cooking Time: 20 mins

Servings: 3

Ingredients

- 2 slices, white bread
- ½ cup, milk

- 8 ounces, beef
- 8 ounces, pork
- ¼ inches, chopped onion
- 3/4 tsp, all spices
- 1, large egg
- Black pepper and salt
- Nonstick cooking spray
- Lingonberry jam

Steps

1. Soak the bread with in milk for about six minutes, then drain off any excess milk. To the bread, add the onion, pork, egg, beef, spices, salt, and pepper. Make tiny balls of the supplied materials.

2. Spray vegetable oil inside the basket of the air fryer and maintain a temperature of 3,600 degrees Fahrenheit until the balls are golden brown; top with the jam.

Nutritional Serving

398 Cal, Protein: 36 g, Carb: 14 g, Fat 14 g

5.13 Air Fryer Fried Shrimp

Preparation Time: 10 mins

Cooking Time: 5 mins

Servings: 3

Ingredients

- Nonstick cooking spray
- 16-20, 1 lb shrimps
- Black pepper n salt
- ½ cup, rice
- 2, large eggs
- 1 cup, panko breadcrumbs
- Fiery remoulade sauce
- ½ cup, mayonnaise
- 2 tsp, diced jalapenos
- 2 tsp, mustard
- 1 tbsp, ketchup
- 1 tbsp, chilli sauce
- 1 piece, scallion

Steps

1. For fried shrimp, coat the basket of a 3.5-quart frying pan with cooking spray and set aside. Pat the shrimp dry with a couple paper towels, then sprinkle with a sprinkle of salt & a few pinches of black pepper.

2. In a mixing bowl, mix the flour, salt, and pepper in a whisk. In a separate small cup, mix together the eggs and a pinch of salt. In a third small dish, panko is placed. Dunk the shrimp in the flour mixture, brush out any excess, then dunk in the egg mixture, dredge in the panko, and toss until finely coated. Follow the above process with the remaining shrimp on a dish or baking sheet with a rim.

3. The air fryer must be heated to 420 ° before use. Working in groups, place a portion of a shrimp in the frying basket in a single layer, and then coat the shrimp lightly with more non-stick cooking spray. Cook for about 10 minutes, flipping the shrimp halfway through, until golden brown and fully done.

4. In a small bowl, combine the mayonnaise, pickled jalapenos, mustard, ketchup, chilli sauce, and scallion until smooth. The sauce should accompany the fried shrimp.

Nutritional Serving

95 Cal, Protein: 10 g, Carb: 12 g, Fat 0 g

5.14 Air Fryer Bread

Preparation Time: 15 mins

Cooking Time: 15 mins

Servings: 4

Ingredients

- 2 tbsp, unsalted butter
- 1 1/2 tsp, dry yeast
- 1 1/2 tsp, Sugar
- 1 1/2 tsp, salt
- 2 2/3 cups, flour

Steps

1. Place the butter in a 6-by-3-inch pan and set it aside.

2. Add the yeast, butter, salt, Sugar, and one cup of warm water to a stand mixer fitted with a dough connector extension. With the mixer machine on a low speed, gradually incorporate flour, waiting until each addition is well incorporated before adding more. When all of the flour is added, mould the dough for 8 minutes under moderate pressure.

3. Transfer the dough to the designated plate, cover the dough, and allow it to rise for around sixty hours, or until it is doubled in size.

4. Attach the Pan to the 3.5-quart air frying pan and set the temperature to 380 degrees Fahrenheit. Cook for about 20 minutes, or until the inside temperature reaches 201 degrees Fahrenheit and the bread is browned. In the Pan, cool for five minutes, then transfer to a shelf to cool completely.

Nutritional Serving

285 Cal, Protein: 16 g, Carb: 18 g, Fat 17 g

5.15 Air Fryer Thanksgiving Turkey

Preparation Time: 15 mins

Cooking Time: 40 mins

Servings: 8

Ingredients

- 1 tsp, Salt
- 1 tsp, Dried Thyme
- 1 tsp, Rosemary
- 1/2 tsp, Black pepper
- 1/2 tsp, Dried sage
- 1/2 tsp, Garlic powder
- 1/2 tsp, Paprika
- 1/2 tsp, Brown sugar
- 2 ½ lbs, Breast of turkey with skin
- Olive oil

Steps

1. Cinnamon, Thyme, rosemary, garlic powder, pepper, sage, brown sugar, and paprika are combined in a small cup.
2. Coat the Breast of turkey with olive oil and coat both sides with the dried buff mixture, ensuring that it penetrates the skin as much as possible. Put the turkey skin-side downwards in the basket of a 3.5-quart air fryer and roast at 365 degrees Fahrenheit for 20 minutes.
3. Carefully open the air frying pan and flip the turkey so that the skin is facing up. Cap the air fryer and roast the meat for about 15 minutes longer, or until an instant-read thermometer inserted into the thickest area of the meat registers 165 degrees F. Allow it to cool down for ten minutes at least prior to slicing and serving.

Nutritional Serving

208 Cal, Protein: 41 g, Carb: 10 g, Fat 4 g

5.16 Air Fryer Frozen Chicken Breast

Preparation Time: 5 mins

Cooking Time: 20 mins

Servings: 30

Ingredients

- Nonstick spray
- Ounces, frozen Breast of boneless chicken
- 1 tsp, olive oil
- Black pepper and salt

Steps

1. Preheat an air fryer of 3.5 quarts to 370 degrees Fahrenheit and coat the basket with nonstick oil.
2. Sprinkle the chicken breast with olive oil. On both sides, liberally sprinkle salt and pepper. Put the chicken in the air fryer basket and cook for 20 - 24 minutes at 365 degrees Fahrenheit.

Nutritional Serving

210 Cal, Protein: 25 g, Carb: 2 g, Fat 10 g

5.17 Air Fryer Banana Bread

Preparation Time: 15 mins

Cooking Time: 15 mins

Servings: 2

Ingredients

- ½ Cup, rice
- ¼ cup, wheat flour or germ
- 1/2 tsp, salt
- 1/4 tsp, baking soda
- 2, bananas
- 1/2 cup, Sugar
- 1/4 cup, vegetable oil
- 1/4 cup, yogurt
- 1/2 tsp, pure vanilla extract
- 1, egg
- 1 - 2 tsp, turbinado sugar

Steps

1. Use non-stick spray to coat an air-frying plate, metal cake pan, or foil sheet with a 7-inch diameter.
2. Combine the rice, salt, nutritional yeast, and baking soda in a medium bowl. In a separate medium-sized cup, puree the bananas until they are quite creamy. Whisk the cream, granulated sugar, milk, vanilla, and egg together with the banana until creamy. Sieve the dry ingredients well over wet and fold with a spoon until barely combined. Using the prepped plate, scrape and smooth the mixture's surface. If necessary, spray the surface of the mixture with turbinado sugar to create a crispy, soft covering.
3. Put the Pan in an air frying pan and cook at 315 °F for 15 to 30 minutes, turning the Pan halfway through, until a toothpick inserted into the middle of the loaf comes out clean. For 10 minutes of cooling, place the Pan on a shelf. Before slicing the banana bread for consumption, knead the dough from the Pan and allow it to cool completely on the shelf.

Nutritional Serving

85 Cal, Protein: 22 g, Carb: 25 g, Fat 1 g

5.18 Air Fryer Veggie Chip Medley

Preparation Time: 14 mins

Cooking Time: 16 mins

Servings: 4

Ingredients

- 4 ounces, sweet potato
- 4 ounces, purple potato
- 2 tbsp, olive oil
- Black pepper and salt
- Ounces, red beet

- Ounces, golden beet

Steps

1. To eliminate the starch from the potato, first, wash and then pat dry the slices until they are 1/14 inch thick.
2. After adding potatoes in a bowl, add salt, oil, and pepper to the bowl.
3. The air frying pan is preheated to 350°F and a capacity of 3.5 quarts. Put the potatoes in layers and heat until golden brown, turning the potatoes every 8 minutes.
4. Then, add it in a second dish and toss it with oil, salt, crushed red pepper, and pepper until it is evenly coated.
5. Add beet chips and potato chips to a plate, sprinkle with salt, and combine. Once it has cooled, it may be stored in a jar.

Nutritional Serving

155 Cal, Protein: 10 g, Carb: 1 g, Fat 11 g

5.19 Air Fryer Spareribs

Preparation Time: 20 mins

Cooking Time: 10 mins

Servings: 4

Ingredients

- Black pepper n salt
- 3 tsp, paprika
- 2 1/2 to 3 pounds, pork ribs
- 2 cups, ketchup
- 1/3 cup, vinegar
- 1/3 cup, white vinegar
- 1/3 cup, brown sugar dark
- 2 tsp, worcestershire sauce
- 1 or 2 tsp, sweet sauce

Steps

1. In a big cup, whisk together a pinch of salt, two tbsp of pepper and 1 tsp of paprika till just mixed. Attach the ribs and swirl to cover, squeezing each rib with the spices.
2. To 325 degrees, preheat a 3.5-quart air fryer. Move the ribs to the fryer basket and cook for around 45 minutes until the ribs are crispy and golden brown.
3. Meanwhile, in a medium-sized saucepan, combine the vinegar, ketchup, white vinegar, Worcestershire, brown Sugar, chili sauce, 2 tbsp of salt, 2 tsp of pepper, 3 cups of water, and the other 2 tbsp of paprika. Cook over medium heat, constantly stirring, for around 2 minutes, until the Sugar is dissolved, and the sauce is cooked through. Cover and put it over low heat.
4. Dip each one into the sauce until the ribs are fried, allowing the surplus runoff. Serve with the leftover sauce.

Nutritional Serving

200 Cal, Protein: 11 g, Carb: 12 g, Fat 13 g

5.20 Homemade Italian meatball air fryer

Preparation Time: 18 mins

Cooking Time: 20 mins

Servings: 3

Ingredients

- 2 lb, ground beef
- 2, big eggs
- 1-1/4 cup, breadcrumbs
- ¼ cup, parsley chopped
- 1 tsp, dried oregano
- ¼ cup, parmigiano reggiano
- 1, small clove of diced garlic
- Black pepper and salt

Steps

1. On a soft cloth, 1 teaspoonful of light oil is sprayed to coat the basket of an air fryer.
2. Place the meat and all of the spices in a large mixing dish.
3. Combine all of the ingredients using your hands. You may begin the mixing process using a wooden utensil, but by using your hands is by far the most efficient method. Combine the materials until all is well blended.
4. Consume a small amount of beef and shape it into a perfect-sized meatball (about 6 mm in diameter) in your palm. Alternately, you may use a biscuit scoop to create identical-sized meatballs.
5. In accordance with the manufacturer's instructions, prepare the Air Fryer. I cover the basket with a tissue aper and drizzle it with avocado oil.
6. At 350 degrees Fahrenheit, cook them for 10 to 13 minutes until they have a light brown colour. Flip the oven and cook for a further 4 to 5 minutes. Place the food on a tray for cooking.
7. When ready to continue cooking, add them to the tomato sauce.
8. Serve with noodles of your choice.

Nutritional Serving

311 Cal, Protein: 15 g, Carb: 12 g, Fat 3 g

5.21 Twice Air Fried Vegan Stuffed Idaho Potatoes

Preparation Time: 15 mins

Cooking Time: 15 mins

Servings: 2

Ingredients

- 2, large potatoes

- 1 - 2 tsp, olive oil
- ¼ cup, unsweetened vegan yogurt
- ¼ cup, milk
- 2 tsp, nutritional yeast
- ½ tsp, salt
- ¼ tsp, pepper
- 1 cup, minced spinach

Optional Ingredients for Topping

- ¼ Cup, unsweetened vegan yogurt
- Smoked pepper and salt
- Parsley chives chopped

Steps

1. On both sides, spray each potato with oil.
2. Preheat your air fryer to 380 °. Add the potatoes to your air-fryer basket until it's warmed.
3. Adjust the cooking time to 40 minutes, change the potatoes over when the Time is finished, and steam for 30 more minutes.
4. Note: You may need to cook an extra 15 - 20 minutes, based on your potatoes' size.
5. Let the potatoes cool so that without burning yourself, you may hold them.
6. Lengthwise, split each potato in half and carefully scoop out the center of the potato, leaving enough to create a stable potato skin shell and a thin layer of the white part.
7. Smoothly mash the scooped potato, organic tofu, honey, natural yeast, salt, and pepper.
8. Mix in the diced spinach, and the mixture can cover the potato shells.
9. Heat for 5 minutes at 325 ° (or near as the air fryer can be mounted to that).
10. Serve and savour with your favourite toppings.

Nutritional Serving

119 Cal, Protein: 2 g, Carb: 20 g, Fat 8 g

5.22 Air Fryer Beef Empanadas

Preparation Time: 15 mins

Cooking Time: 10 mins

Servings: 4

Ingredients

- 8, discs of goya empanada
- 1 cup, picadillo
- 1, white egg
- 1 tsp, water

Steps

1. Heat the air frying pan to 325F for 8 minutes. Cover the basket lightly with frying oil.
2. Place two tablespoons of picadillo with in the center of each tortilla disc. Fold it in

116

halves and use a fork to seal the edges. Repeat with the remaining dough.

3. Add water to the whites of the eggs before rubbing the empanadas' edges.

4. Cook 2 - 3 at a time in an air frying pan for eight minutes, until golden brown. Turn down the heat and continue with the remaining empanadas.

Nutritional Serving

155 Cal, Protein: 20 g, Carb: 12 g, Fat 10 g

5.23 Healthy Fish Finger Sandwich & Optimum Healthy Air Fry

Preparation Time: 15 mins

Cooking Time: 15 mins

Servings: 6

Ingredients

- 4, tiny cod fillets
- Pepper and salt
- 2 tbsp, flour
- 40 g, dry breadcrumbs
- Oil spray
- 250 g, frozen peas
- 1 tbsp, crème fraiche
- 10-12, capers
- Lemon juice
- 4, bread rolls

Steps

1. Preheating the Air Fryer is the first step.

2. Season each fish fillet with salt and pepper and lightly dust with flour. Then quickly roll in breadcrumbs. The goal is to get a thin coating of breadcrumbs rather than a thick one. Repeat with each fish fillet.

3. Apply two spritz of oil mist to the fryer basket's perimeter. Add the cod fillets & cook for 15 minutes on the fish option (200c).

4. While the fish is frying, cook the chickpeas in the boiling water for several moments on the stovetop or in the oven. Drain, then combine the capers, crème fraiche, and lemon juice to taste in a blender. Once combined, pulverise thoroughly.

5. Until the fish is done, remove the sandwich from Air Fryer and begin stacking the bread, fish, and pea puree. Additionally, lettuce, tartar sauce, and your preferred condiments may be added.

Nutritional Serving

788 Cal, Protein: 20 g, Carb: 21 g, Fat 16 g

5.24 Quinoa Burgers Air fryer

Preparation Time: 20 mins

Cooking Time: 15 mins

Servings: 5

Ingredients

- 1 cup, crimson
- 1-1/2 cup, water
- 1 tsp, salt
- Black pepper
- 1-1/2 cups, rolled oats
- 3, eggs
- ¼ cup, white onion
- ½ cup, crumbled feta cheese
- ¼ cup, chopped fresh chives
- Black pepper and salt
- Palm oil
- 4, whole-wheat hamburgers buns
- 4, arugulas
- 4 slices, tomato

Yogurt dill sauce with cucumber

- 1 cup, diced cucumber
- 1 cup, Greek yogurt
- 2 tbsp, lemon extract
- ¼ tsp, salt
- Black pepper
- 1 tbsp, fresh dill minced
- 1 tbsp, olive oil

Steps

1. Prepare the quinoa: In a skillet, rinse the quinoa in cold water and stir until some dry husks rise to the surface. Drain the quinoa as much as possible, then set the pot on the stove. On the burner, raise the temperature to medium-high and dry the quinoa by shaking the Pan intermittently until the quinoa moves rapidly and that you can listen the seeds moving. Add the water, pepper, and salt to the dish. Bringing the mixture to a boil, then reduce the heat to medium or medium-low. You need only see two bubbles, not really a boil. Top it with a cover, tilt it slightly, or merely set the lid down on the pot if it has spouts, and bring it to a boil for twenty minutes. Put out the flames and fluff the quinoa with a fork. If the bottom of the pot still has liquid, place it back on the heat for another three minutes or so. Distribute evenly the cooked quinoa on a sheet plate to cool.

2. In a large bowl, combine room-temperature quinoa, eggs, oats, cheese, onion, and seasonings. Season with pepper and salt, then mix well. Form four patties from the mixture. To get the proper consistency for forming patties, add a little amount of water or a few more rolled oats.

3. You may need to cook these burgers in many batches, based on the size of your air fryer. Air-fry every batch at 400°F for 10 minutes, turning the patties halfway through the cooking process.

4. Prepare the cucumber yogurt dill sauce while the burgers are cooking by combining all of the ingredients in a cup.

5. On whole-wheat hamburger buns, top your burger with onion, arugula, and cucumber yogurt dill sauce.

Nutritional Serving

122 Cal, Protein: 25 g, Carb: 12 g, Fat 16 g

5.25 Air Fryer Pepperoni Pizza

Preparation Time: 15 mins

Cooking Time: 20 mins

Servings: 4

Ingredients

- 1, Pita wheat
- 2 tbsp, pizza or marinara sauce
- 1/8 cup, mozzarella cheese sliced
- 1/8 cup, cheddar cheese
- ¼ cup, mozzarella cheese
- 8, pepperoni slices
- Olive oil spray
- 1 tbsp, chopped parsley

Steps

1. Spread the sauce over the pita bread, then layer the pepperoni and grated cheese on top.

2. Using olive oil spritz to coat the pizza's surface.

3. Place this inside the Air Fryer at 400 degrees for 10 minutes. Check the pizza after six to seven minutes to ensure it has not overcooked.

4. Remove the pizza from the Air Fryer.

Before serving Instructions

1. For a crispier exterior, spritz one side of the flatbread with olive oil. Place this inside the Air Fryer at 400 degrees for four minutes. It will be simpler to crisp one side of the pita.

2. Now remove the pita bread from the Air Fryer. Place the pita on the side that is less crunchy. That should be the Air Fryer's hand that was inverted.

3. Drizzle the pizza with sauce and top with pepperoni and cheese slices.

4. Put the pizza back into the Air Fryer for 3 to 4 minutes, or until the cheese has melted. To reach the ideal texture, you may need to cook the pizza for a few more minutes.

5. Then remove the pizza from the Air Fryer using a spoon. Serve with pleasure.

Nutritional Serving

351 Cal, Protein: 20 g, Carb: 11 g, Fat 15 g

5.26 Crispy air fryer Tofu along with sticky orange sauce

Preparation Time: 20 mins

Cooking Time: 10 mins

Servings: 6

Ingredients

- 1 lb, tofu extra-firm
- 1 tbsp, tamari
- 1 tbsp, cornstarch

For the sauce

- 1 tsp, orange zest
- 1/3 cup, orange juice
- ½ cup, water
- 2 tsp, cornstarch
- ¼ tsp, smashed red pepper flakes
- 1 tsp, minced ginger
- 1 tsp, minced garlic
- 1 tsp, maple syrup

Steps

1. Slice the tofu cubes.
2. Place the tofu cubes in a plastic storage bag of quart size. Add the tamari and shut the container. Shake the bag, so the tamari is evenly distributed throughout the tofu.
3. Fill the container with 1 teaspoon of cornstarch. Shake again until the tofu is evenly distributed. Tofu should be marinated for at least fifteen minutes.
4. In the meanwhile, mix the ingredients for the sauce in a small bowl using a spoon.
5. Place the tofu in an air fryer in a single layer.
6. Cook the tofu at 390 degrees for ten minutes, shaking after 5 minutes.
7. After the tofu has been prepared, add the other ingredients to a pan over medium heat. The sauce is swirled and then poured over the tofu. Stir the tofu and sauce together until the sauce thickens & the tofu is cooked.
8. Serve immediately with rice and steaming veggies, if desired.

Nutritional Serving

155 Cal, Protein: 12 g, Carb: 11 g, Fat 3 g

5.27 Bourbon Bacon Burger

Preparation Time: 25 mins

Cooking Time: 15 mins

Servings: 1

Ingredients

- 1 tbsp, whiskey

- 2 tbsp, brown Sugar
- 3, half-slices of maple bacon strips
- ¾ pound, 80% ground beef
- 1 tbsp, minced onion
- 2 tsp, BBQ sauce
- ½ tsp, salt
- Black pepper
- 2, Monterey jack or colby jack cheese slices
- 2, kaiser rolls
- Lettuce and tomato for serving

Zesty Sauce for Burger

- 2 tsp, BBQ sauce
- 2 tsp, mayonnaise
- ¼ tsp, paprika field
- Black pepper

Steps

1. Preheat the air fryer to 390° Fahrenheit and add a little amount of water to the bottom tray. (This would prevent the oil that drops through the rear drawer from igniting and smoking.)
2. In a shallow glass, combine the whiskey and brown Sugar. Put the bacon strips in the air fryer dish and massage them well with brown sugar mixture. Four-hour air-frying at 390°F. Add more brown Sugar, flip the bacon, and air-fry it at 390 degrees Fahrenheit for an additional four minutes.
3. Prepare the burger patties while the bacon cooks. Combine the BBQ sauce, ground beef, pepper, cabbage, and salt in a large bowl. Mix with your hands and shape the meat into two buns.
4. Depending on the desired doneness (15 minutes for rare to intermediate), transfer the patties to the air frying basket & cook at 370°F for 20 minutes. Halfway through the cooking period, flip the hamburgers.
5. In a bowl, combine mayonnaise, barbecue sauce, paprika, and black pepper according to taste to create burger sauce.
6. Top each patty with a piece of Colby Jack cheese & air-fry for an additional minute, until the patties reach the desired doneness, in order to melt the cheese. Spread the sauce on the buns, place the burgers on the rolls, and top with lettuce, tomato, and bourbon bacon.

Nutritional Serving

665 Cal, Protein: 41 g, Carb: 70 g, Fat 11 g

5.28 Leftover Greek Spanakopita Pie in The Air Fryer

Preparation Time: 23 mins

Cooking Time: 25 mins

Servings: 6

Ingredients

- Turkey Leftover Chopped Brown Meat
- Pastry
- 2, big Eggs
- 1, Tiny Egg for brushing the pastries
- 200 g, Spinach
- 1, big Onion
- 2, big Eggs
- 250g, Cream Cheese
- 100 g, Feta Cheese
- 1 tsp, Basil
- 1 tbsp, Oregano
- 1 tbsp, Thyme
- Pepper & salt

Steps

1. Remove the leftover veggies from the fridge and season them thoroughly with salt and pepper.
2. Place the vegetables in a tea cloth and squeeze off any excess liquid. Combine them with the spices and feta in a mixing bowl.
3. Combine the soft cheese and egg until the mixture is light and airy.
4. Put and apply the batter to a filo pastry plate until it is three-quarters full. Cover the majority of the pastry with the whisked egg.
5. Air-fry for 20 minutes at 180 degrees Celsius.

Nutritional Serving

110 Cal, Protein: 3 g, Carb: 34 g, Fat 24 g

5.29 Tandoori chicken

Preparation Time: 15 mins

Cooking Time: 15 mins

Servings: 12

Ingredients

- 4, thigh chicken legs

Steps for the first margination

- 1 tsp, salt
- 2 tsp, lemon extract
- 2 tsp, paste of ginger garlic
- 1 tsp, red pepper powder

For the second margination

- 2 tbsp, curd
- 1 tsp, ginger garlic
- 1 tsp, red pepper powder
- ½ tsp, powder of black pepper
- ½ tsp, turmeric powder
- ½ tsp, cumin powder
- 1 tsp, coriander powder

- 2 tbsp, mustard oil
- Lemon juice
- 2 tsp, cream

Steps

1. Wash the chicken and, using a sharp knife, make three to four small holes on each piece.
2. Mix the ingredients for the 1st marinade and apply them carefully to the chicken legs.
3. Cover the dish and chill for 5 to 6 hours.
4. Cover the chicken with the materials for the 2nd marinade in a dish.
5. Cover and chill the bowl for a further four to five hours.
6. Preheat oven to 178 ° C.
7. Place the drip tray in the lower portion of the air frying oven.
8. Place a wire rack on top of the drip tray.
9. Prepare the chicken for twenty minutes on a cooling rack before grilling.
10. Again, grill the chicken legs for 15 to 20 minutes, until they are fully done.
11. Butter should be used to baste the chicken while cooking.
12. Remove and thoroughly clean the air frying oven.
13. Serve and consume with lemons.

Nutritional Serving

112 Cal, Protein: 10 g, Carb: 15 g, Fat 14 g

5.30 Air Fryer Chicken Nuggets

Preparation Time: 20 mins

Cooking Time: 10 mins

Servings: 4

Ingredients

- 1, Deboned skinless chicken breast
- ¼ tsp, Salt
- 1/8 tsp, Black pepper
- ½ cup, unsalted butter melted
- ½ cup, Breadcrumbs
- 2 tsp, Grated parmesan

Steps

1. Preheat the air fryer to 395 degrees for four minutes.
2. Split the chicken breast fat into 1 1/2-inch thick slices, then cut each slice into two to three nuggets. Combine the pepper and salt with the chicken.
3. Place the melted butter in a small bowl as well as the breadcrumbs (with cheese, if using) in another small dish.
4. Coat each piece of chicken with butter, then breadcrumbs.

5. Place a single batch layer in the air fryer's basket. Based upon the size of the air fryer, you may have to bake in many stages.
6. Set the timer to eight minutes.
7. Upon completion, ensure that the chicken nuggets have had an internal temperature in the range of 165 degrees Fahrenheit. Using chopsticks, remove nuggets from the basket and place them on a pan to cool.

Nutritional Serving

168 Cal, Protein: 14 g, Carb: 41 g, Fat 45 g

5.31 Air Fryer Ranch Chicken Tenders

Preparation Time: 15 mins

Cooking Time: 10 mins

Servings: 4

Ingredients

- 8, chicken tenders
- Spray canola

For Dredge

- 1 cup, breadcrumbs
- 1, egg
- 2 tbsp, water

For the Seasoning of Ranch Chicken

- ½ Tsp, salt
- ¼ tsp, black pepper
- ½ tsp, garlic powder
- ½ tsp, onion powder
- ¼ tsp, paprika
- 1 tsp, parsley

Steps

1. Allow the Air Fryer to heat it. Set an air fryer at 375 degrees Fahrenheit for five minutes. Allow it to run around without food in the basket.
2. Establish a location for dredging. In a small-sized bowl, mix the egg and water. In a second shallow dish, thoroughly combine the panko breadcrumbs.
3. Prepare the Ranch's seasonings. Combine all ranch seasoning ingredients in a small bowl.
4. For the chicken sauce, spread the ranch seasoning over the chicken tenders in a rotating motion, ensuring that both ends are coated.
5. Soak the tenders of the chicken in the egg wash and then press them into the panko. Turn each side to coat.
6. Load the fryer's basket with food. Place the breaded tenders into the fry basket. Repeat with the remaining bids. In batches, frying may be necessary.
7. Place the Fry Basket inside of the Power Air Fryer. Spray the panko with a thin coating of canola oil cooking spray. Select

the M. The scroll button is lowered to 415 degrees Fahrenheit when the Control button is pressed. Adjust its cooking time to twelve minutes at 415 degrees. Halfway through cooking, flip the tenders to brown the other side. The tenders are cooked when the center of the fattiest area of the tender reaches 165 degrees Fahrenheit, the flesh is not pink anymore, as well as the fluids run clear.

Nutritional Serving

500 Cal, Protein: 15 g, Carb: 23 g, Fat 8 g

5.32 Air fryer beef

Preparation Time: 15 mins

Cooking Time: 20 mins

Servings: 6

Ingredients

- Air fryer
- Grill Air frying Pan
- Knife
- Cling Film
- Homemade Pate of Chicken Liver
- Homemade Short crust Pastry
- Beef Fillet
- 1, medium Egg
- Pepper and Salt

Steps

1. Take a piece of beef, clean it, trim any visible fat, season it with pepper and salt, then, it must be wrapped in plastic wrap and refrigerated for one hour.
2. With your batch, make pate of chicken liver and homemade buttercream pastry.
3. To keep it wet for wrapping, roll out the short-crust dough and coat the edges with beaten egg using a pastry brush.
4. Place a thin coating of the prepared pate inside the outside egg line, and the white sausage will no longer be visible.
5. Peel away wrap off the pork, then set the meat atop of the pate in the tart's center and pressing it down.
6. Enclose the meat as well as the pate with the pastry.
7. Give the pastry a high rating so that the meat may thrive.
8. Put the Air fryer upon the Air fryer Grill Pan & cook for 30 minutes at 165°C/325°F.
9. Allow it rest for a few minutes before slicing and serving with roast potatoes.

Nutritional Serving

250 Cal, Protein: 50 g, Carb: 5 g, Fat 5 g

5.33 Air Fryer Falafel

Preparation Time: 15 mins

Cooking Time: 10 mins

Servings: 8

Ingredients

- 15.5 ounces, Chickpeas
- 1, small Onion
- 3, Garlic cloves
- 1/3 cup, Parsley
- 1/3 cup, Cilantro
- 1/3 cup, Scallions
- 1 tsp, Cumin
- ½ tsp, Salt
- 1/8 tsp, Crushed red pepper flakes
- 1 tsp, baking Powder
- 4 tsp, Flour
- Olive oil

Steps

1. Rinse the chickpeas on paper towels.
2. Place the garlic and onions in the food processor or blender fitted with a steel blade. Add parsley, scallion, cumin, coriander, red pepper flakes, and garlic.
3. Process for 30 to 60 seconds until combined, then add chickpeas & pulse 3 to 4 times until combined, but not pureed.
4. Spray the sides of the dish with baking powder & flour, combine with a spatula, and pulse two or three times.
5. Transfer to a bowl, cover, and let to cool for 3 to 4 hours.
6. If the dough is too sticky, add extra flour to your fingertips and cutting board and roll it into 12 balls.
7. Preheat the Air Fryer to 350°F.
8. Oil the falafel and sprinkle it with oil. Cook in portions for 14 minutes, flipping halfway through, until golden brown.

Nutritional Serving

395 Cal, Protein: 40 g, Carb: 5 g, Fat 9 g

5.34 Air Fryer Bacon Burger Bites

Preparation Time: 30 mins

Cooking Time: 10 mins

Servings: 4

Ingredients

- 2 lbs, cattle
- 4 oz, raw bacon
- 2 tsp, mustard
- ½ tsp, salt
- ½ tsp, onion powder
- ¼ tsp, black pepper
- 1, butter lettuce

- 30, tomatoes
- 30, thin slices of jalapeño
- 30, dill pickle slices
- Mayo, yellow mustard, and ketchup

Steps

1. With your fingers, combine the beef, mustard, pork, cinnamon, onion powder, and pepper.
2. formed into thirty tennis balls sized.
3. Preheat the Air Fryer to 400°F. In batches, hamburgers are placed in a single layer.
4. Cook, flipping halfway, to the desired level of potency for 10 to 15 minutes.
5. Place any burger on a skewer with lettuce, pickles, and tomatoes, and serve with condiments.

Nutritional Serving

250 Cal, Protein: 25 g, Carb: 20 g, Fat 10 g

5.35 Air Fryer Bacon Wrapped Scallops

Preparation Time: 60 mins

Cooking Time: 10 mins

Servings: 3

Ingredients

- 16, large sea scallops
- 8, bacon centrally sliced
- 16, toothpicks
- Olive oil
- Black pepper

Steps

1. Preheat the air fryer to 402 degrees Fahrenheit for three minutes.
2. To partially cook the bacon for three minutes, place it in an air fryer and flip it halfway through. Remove and place on a tissue paperto cool.
3. Remove any side muscles from the scallops. The scallops must be patted dry with tissue paper to remove any moisture.
4. Every scallop is wrapped with bacon, and a toothpick is used to secure it.
5. The scallops are delicately seasoned with black pepper and brushed with olive oil.
6. Arrange scallops in the air fryer in a single layer and roast for 8 minutes, until the scallops are tender and transparent and the pork is cooked through.

Nutritional Serving

450 Cal, Protein: 20 g, Carb: 41 g, Fat 8.3 g

5.36 Air Fryer Chicken Milanese With Arugula

Preparation Time: 15 mins

Cooking Time: 10 mins

Servings: 3

Ingredients

- 16 oz, skinless, deboned chicken breasts
- ¾ tsp, salt
- Black pepper
- ½ cup, seasoned wheat or gluten-free whole wheat breadcrumbs
- 2 tsp, parmesan cheese
- 1, egg
- Olive oil spray
- 6, arugula cup infants
- 3 slices, lemon wedges

Steps

1. Cut the chicken into four fillets, place them between two sheets of paper towel or plastic wrap, and pound them to a thickness of half an inch.
2. Sprinkle pepper and salt on both ends.
3. In a small basin, whisk the egg & 1 teaspoon of water together.
4. In a small-sized bowl, mix the breadcrumbs and parmesan cheese.
5. Coat the chicken with egg, followed by the breadcrumb mixture. Put it on a work surface and spritz both sides with olive oil.
6. Warm the air fryer to 402 degrees Fahrenheit for air.
7. Transfer in batches to the air frying basket and cook for 8 minutes, flipping halfway through, until golden and cooked through.
8. Serve the chicken with 1 1/2 cups of arugula and a liberal amount of lemon juice.

Nutritional Serving

456 Cal, Protein: 15 g, Carb: 10 g, Fat 7 g

5.37 Air Fryer Asian Glazed Boneless Chicken Thighs

Preparation Time: 25 mins

Cooking Time: 30 mins

Servings: 6

Ingredients

- 32 ounces, 8 deboned chicken thighs
- ¼ cup, soy sauce with sodium
- 2-1/2 tsp, Balsamic vinegar
- 1 tbsp, Honey
- 3, Garlic cloves
- 1 tsp, Sriracha sauce
- 1 tsp, grated ginger fresh
- 1, scallion green and sliced for garnish

Steps

1. In a small bowl, thoroughly combine the soy sauce, balsamic wine, Sugar, garlic, ginger, and sriracha.

2. Place half (1/4 cup) of the mixture into a big chicken dish, coat the meat with it, and marinate for at least 2 hours or overnight, if possible.
3. Save the excess sauce for later use.
4. Preheat the fryer for air to 400 degrees Fahrenheit.
5. Remove the chicken from the marinade & put it in the air fryer's basket.
6. Cook in portions for fifteen minutes, turning halfway through, until well done.
7. Meanwhile, place the remaining sauce in a small saucepan and boil over moderate heat until reduced and thickened, about 2 minutes.
8. To serve, sprinkle the sauce over the chicken and garnish with scallions.

Nutritional Serving

199 Cal, Protein: 15 g, Carb: 16 g, Fat 20 g

5.38 Air Fryer Cajun Shrimp Dinner

Preparation Time: 20 mins

Cooking Time: 25 mins

Servings: 8

Ingredients

- 1 tbsp, creole or Cajun
- 1 lb, 24 extra jumbo shrimps
- 6 ounces, turkey
- 1, medium zucchini
- 8 ounces, medium yellow squash
- 1, large bell pepper red
- ¼ tsp, salt
- 2 tsp, olive oil

Steps

1. In a large bowl, combine the Cajun spice and shrimp, then toss to coat.
2. With the oil, combine the zucchini, bacon, salt, squash, and bell peppers.
3. Heat the Air Fryer to 402 degrees Fahrenheit.
4. Transfer the shrimp and veggies to the air fryer basket in 2 rounds (for small baskets) & cook for 10 minutes, turning the basket between three and four times.
5. Repeat with the remaining shrimp and veggies.
6. When all batches have been fried, return the 1st portion to the air fryer and cook for an additional minute.

Nutritional Serving

250 Cal, Protein: 20 g, Carb: 15 g, Fat 10 g

5.39 Easy Garlic Knots

Preparation Time: 30 mins

Cooking Time: 15 mins

Servings: 4

Ingredients

- Spritz with olive oil
- 1 cup, whole wheat flour white
- ¾ tsp, Salt
- 2 tbsp, Baking powder
- 1 cup, Greek Yogurt
- 2 tbsp, Butter
- 3, Garlic cloves
- 1 tbsp, parmesan cheese grated
- 1 tbsp, Parsley

Steps

1. Oven to 450 degrees Fahrenheit. Cover a perforated baking sheet with a silicone liner or Silpat.
2. In a large mixing basin, combine the rice, baking powder, and salt. Blend the yogurt with a spoon after it's all incorporated. Knead the dough approximately fifteen times with your dry hands. If it's becoming too sloppy, add a bit more flour. Make a ball out of it.
3. Divide the material into 8 equal halves, and roll each slice into worm-like segments, approximately 9 inches long.
4. Roll each breadstick it into "knot-like" ball and place on the prepared baking pan.
5. Cook in the upper third of oven for about 20 minutes, or until brown. Allow for a five-minute cooling period.
6. In a medium nonstick pan, melt the butter, add the garlic, and cook for 2 minutes, or until golden.
7. Toss the knots in Pan with the melted butter and garlic, or use a spatula to coat the garlic knots.
8. If the tangles are too dry, give them another spray of olive oil. Scatter with parmesan cheese and cut parsley.

Nutritional Serving

399 Cal, Protein: 15 g, Carb: 16 g, Fat 10 g

5.40 Tostones (Twice air-fried plantains)

Preparation Time: mins

Cooking Time: mins

Servings:

Ingredients

- 6 oz, Green plantain
- Spritz olive oil
- 1 cup, Water
- 1 tsp, Salt
- ¾ tsp, Garlic

Steps

1. Divide the plantain into eight one-inch slices.
2. Mix the water, salt, and garlic powder in a shallow cup.
3. Preheat the air fryer to 400°F.
4. You'll have to do this in different sessions if you can spritz the plantain using olive oil & cook it for six minutes.
5. When they are sweet, remove them from the air fryer and place them in a measuring cup for flattening.
6. Soak them in seasoned water and set them aside.
7. Prepare the air fryer at 400 degrees F and cook the plantains in rounds for five minutes on each side, spraying both sides with olive oil.
8. When you're done, give them another spray of oil and some salt. Eat as soon as possible.

Nutritional Serving

166 Cal, Protein: 8 g, Carb: 55 g, Fat 30 g

5.41 Stuffed Bagel Balls

Preparation Time: 26 mins

Cooking Time: 10 mins

Servings: 3

Ingredients

- 1 cup, Rice
- 2 tsp, Baking powder
- ¾ tsp, Salt
- 1 cup, Yogurt
- Box of fat cream cheese cut into eight pieces 4 tsp. and 4 oz.
- 1, beaten egg white

Steps

1. Spray the basket to keep it from sticking.
2. Preheat the Air Fryer to 320°F. Bake for 9 to 10 minutes, or until golden, in non-overcrowded batches.
3. There's no need to take turns. Allow ten minutes for cooling at least before eating.

Nutritional Serving

199 Cal, Protein: 20 g, Carb: 11 g, Fat 16 g

5.42 Za'atar lamb chops

Preparation Time: 20 mins

Cooking Time: 15 mins

Servings: 2

Ingredients

- 8 bone-in lamb loin chops, each trimmed and weighing about 3.5 ounces.
- 3, crushed garlic cloves

- 1 tsp, olive oil extra-virgin
- ½ tsp, lemon
- 1-1/4 tsp, salt
- 1 tbsp, za'atar's
- Ground pepper

Steps

1. Massage the lamb chops with oil and garlic.
2. Pinch the lemon on both ends and season with salt, zaatar, & black pepper.
3. Preheat the air fryer to 402 degrees F. Cook in batches on an even sheet until desired flavour is achieved, about 4 to 5 minutes on each side.
4. According to the nutritional information, each bone has 12 to 2 oz. of uncooked beef on it.

Nutritional Serving

855 Cal, Protein: 69 g, Carb: 12 g, Fat 13 g

5.43 Air Fryer Meatballs

Preparation Time: 30 mins

Cooking Time: 10 mins

Servings: 6

Ingredients

- 16 ounces, ground leaf
- 4 ounces, ground pork
- 1 tsp, italian seasoning
- 1/2tsp, salt
- 2, garlic cloves
- ½ cup, parmesan cheese
- 1, egg
- 1/3 cup, breadcrumbs italian seasoned

Steps

1. Preheat an air fryer to 350°F.
2. In a large mixing bowl, mix all of the materials and use an ice cream cone to form 16 meatballs.
3. Heat 12 of the meatballs in air fryer for 8 minutes. Cook for a further 2 minutes after moving the bowl. Transfer the meatballs to a new tray and continue the process with the remaining meatballs.

Nutritional Serving

660 Cal, Protein: 29 g, Carb: 31 g, Fat 10 g

5.44 Air Fryer Salmon Patties

Preparation Time: 15 mins

Cooking Time: 8 mins

Servings: 4

Ingredients

- ½ Cup, mayonnaise
- 1 tsp, minced garlic
- ½ tsp, lemon

- 2, pinches of cajun seasoning

Patties

- 12 ounces, salmon
- 1 tbsp, fresh chives
- 1 tsp, dried parsley
- ½ tsp, salt
- ½ tsp, minced garlic
- 1 tbsp, flour
- Cooking spray
- 1, lemon

Steps

1. Combine the mayonnaise, garlic, Cajun spice, and lemon juice in a small cup and chill until ready to use.
2. In a medium mixing bowl, combine the chives, salmon, parsley, garlic, and salt. Remove the flour & thoroughly combine. Form into patties by dividing the mixture into four equal halves.
3. Preheat the air fryer to 175°C. Using a knife, cut the lemon into 4 slices.
4. Cover the lemon segments in the bottom of air fryer dish with salmon patties. Coat the patties lightly with cooking spray.
5. Place the bowl in preheated fryer and lower the heat to 135 degrees Celsius.
6. Cook in air fryer for 15 minutes, or until a thermometer placed in the centre of a patty registers 145 degrees F. (63 degrees C). Serve with the sauce.

Nutritional Serving

450 Cal, Protein: 15 g, Carb: 10 g, Fat 2 g

5.45 Air Fryer Salmon

Preparation Time: 16 mins

Cooking Time: 15 mins

Servings: 6

Ingredients

- 2, salmon fillets
- Black pepper and salt
- 2 tsp, olive oil
- 2 tbsp, mustard whole grain
- 1 tbsp, brown Sugar
- 1, minced garlic clove
- ½ tsp, thyme leaves

Steps

1. Powder the salmon with pepper and salt all over. Whisk the mustard, oil, Sugar, Thyme, and garlic together in a tiny dish. Spread the salmon on the surface.
2. Organize a bowl of salmon in an air fryer. Set the air fryer to 400°, then cook for 9-10 minutes.

Nutritional Serving

168 Cal, Protein: 19 g, Carb: 25 g, Fat 12 g

5.46 Crispy Parmesan Crusted Chicken Breasts

Preparation Time: 18 mins

Cooking Time: 20 mins

Servings: 8

Ingredients

- Cooking spray
- ½ cup, panko breadcrumbs
- 1/3 cup, parmesan cheese
- ¼ tsp, paprika
- ¼ tsp, salt
- ¼ tsp, black pepper ground
- 3 tbsp, melted butter
- 2 tsp, white wine
- 1 tsp, dijon mustard
- 1, garlic clove

Steps

1. The air frying oven is heated to 200 degrees Celsius. Line a baking pan with aluminum foil and coat it with cooking spray.
2. Combine the breadcrumbs, parmesan cheese, salt, paprika, and black pepper in a small bowl. In a separate cup, combine the garlic, sugar, white wine, & mustard.
3. 1/2 of each Breast of chicken is dipped in a mixture of melted butter before being evenly coated in a bread crumb batter. Place a single layer of breaded chicken on the baking sheet that has been prepped. The chicken breasts should be coated with the leftover bread crumb mixture.
4. In a preheated oven, roast the chicken for approximately 20 minutes, or until the center is not pink anymore and the juices flow clear.

Nutritional Serving

188 Cal, Protein: 15 g, Carb: 11 g, Fat 7 g

Chapter 6: Desserts Recipes

6.1 Air Fryer Oreos

Preparation Time: 10 mins

Cooking Time: 15 mins

Servings: 2

Ingredients

- ½ cup, Pancake
- 1/3 cup, water
- Cooking spray
- 9, Chocolate cookies
- 1 tbsp, sugar

Steps

1. Combine the pancakes and water in a blender and mix until smooth.
2. Using parchment sheets, line an air fryer bowl. Dip each cookie in the pancake mixture and place it in the bowl. Make absolutely sure they do not even hit them and cook in batches if possible.
3. Preheat the air fryer to 400 degrees Fahrenheit. Cook for 5-6 minutes with the bowl, then switch and cook for another 2 to 3 minutes until lightly browned. Confectioners' sugar is sprinkled on top.

Nutritional Serving

145 Cal, Protein: 98 g, Carb: 44 g, Fat 25g

6.2 Air Fryer Roasted Bananas

Preparation Time: 20 mins

Cooking Time: 60 mins

Servings: 24

Ingredients

- 1/8-inch, banana (sliced)
- Cooking spray

Steps

1. Preheat an air fryer to 375 degrees F.
2. Place banana slices in the basket, so they don't touch; if necessary, cook in batches. Avocado oil should be sprayed on the banana slices.
3. Cook for five min in an air fryer. Carefully chop the banana slices into the basket & rotate them until they are tender. First, before banana slices are roasted and

caramelized, cook for about 2 - 3 mins. Remove it from the basket with care.

Nutritional Serving

200 Cal, Protein: 100 g, Carb: 49 g, Fat 34g

6.3 Air Fryer Beignets

Preparation Time: 20 mins

Cooking Time: 20 mins

Servings: 5

Ingredients

- ½ Cup, flour
- Cooking spray
- 1/8 cup, water
- ¼ cup, sugar
- 1, egg large
- 1 ½ tsp, butter
- ½ tsp, baking powder
- ½ tsp, vanilla extract
- 1 pinch, salt
- 2 tbsp, sugar

Steps

1. Preheat the air-freezer to 185°C.
2. Whisk together all the egg yolk, wheat, water, salt, baking powder, butter, sugar, & vanilla extract in a large mixing bowl. To combine the ingredients, stir them together.
3. In a small bowl, beat white egg at medium speed with an electric hand mixer until soft peaks form. Undersold the batter. Apply batter to filled pot using a little hinged ice cream scoop.
4. In air fryer's basket, place the silicone that has been filled.
5. In a hot oven air fryer, cook for 10 minutes. Remove the mold from the bowl with care, then remove the beignets and flip more than a paper ring.
6. Place the round parchment containing the beignets immediately into the air fryer's bowl. Cook for a further 4 minutes. Take the beignets out from of the air fryer's basin and sprinkle with confectioners' sugar.

Nutritional Serving

190 Cal, Protein: 122 g, Carb: 85g, Fat 25g

6.4 Air-Fried Butter Cake

Preparation Time: 10 mins

Cooking Time: 30 mins

Servings: 4

Ingredients

- 7 tbsp, butter
- Cooking spray
- ¼ cup, sugar
- 2 tbsp, white sugar
- 1, large egg
- 1 2/3 cup, flour
- 6 tbsp, milk
- 1 pinch, salt

Steps

1. With an air fryer, heat to 350 degrees F. Spray a small fluted tube plate with cooking spray.
2. Under a bowl, pound the butter & 1/4 cup 2 tbsp sugar together with an electric mixer until light and creamy. Mix in the egg until it is soft and creamy. Combine the salt & starch in a mixing bowl. Mix in the milk until the batter is entirely combined. Cook the batter in the pan, levelling the top with wooden spoon.
3. Place the pan inside the air fryer's basket. Set a timer for 15 minutes. Bake until a toothpick inserted into the center of the cake comes out clear.
4. Remove the cake from the pan and set aside to cool for about 5 minutes.

Nutritional Serving

120 Cal, Protein: 89 g, Carb: g, Fat g

6.5 House Gluten-Free Fresh Cherry Crumble

Preparation Time: 10 mins

Cooking Time: 25 mins

Servings: 2

Ingredients

- 1/3 cup, butter
- 3 cups, cherries
- 10 tbsp, white sugar
- 2 tsp, lemon
- 1 cup, flour
- 1 tsp, vanilla powder
- 1 tsp, nutmeg
- 1 tsp, cinnamon

Steps

1. Preheat the air-freezer to 165°C.
2. Combine the crushed cherries, lemon juice, and 2 tbsp sugar in a cup and stir well. Fill the baking bowl with the cherry mixture.
3. Combine the flour and 6 tbsp sugar in a cup. Crack the butter with your hands till the flakes resemble pea-size. Remove the

cherries from the jar and carefully press them back into place.

4. 2 tablespoons sugar, nutmeg, vanilla essence, and cinnamon in a cup Over the flour & cherries, sprinkle the sugar coating.

5. In a preheated air fryer, bake the chicken. Check after 24 minutes; if not golden brown, continue cooking and check at 5-minute intervals until golden brown. Close the drawer and switch off the air fryer. Allow 10 minutes for it to collapse within. Allow to cool for about 5 minutes after stirring.

Nutritional Serving

458 Cal, Protein: 32 g, Carb: 32 g, Fat 22 g

6.6 Chocolate Cake in an Air Fryer

Preparation Time: 15 mins

Cooking Time: 20 mins

Servings: 9

Ingredients

- ¼ Cup, white sugar
- 3 ½ tbsp, butter
- 1, large egg
- Cooking spray
- 1 tbsp, apricot jam
- 1 tbsp, flour
- 1 tbsp, cocoa powder
- Salt

Steps

1. With an air fryer, heat to 320 degrees F. Spraying a small, fluted tube plate with cooking spray.

2. In a mixing bowl, pound the butter & sugar together with an electric mixer until frothy and smooth. Blend in the jam and the egg until well combined. Blend in the rice, salt, & cocoa powder until well combined. Pour the mixture into the previously filled pan. Level top of a batter with the wooden spoon.

3. Place the pan inside the air fryer's basket. Cook for 15 minutes or until a toothpick inserted in the center of the cake comes out clean.

Nutritional Serving

222 Cal, Protein: 17 g, Carb: 3 g, Fat 15 g

6.7 Air Fryer Sweet French Toast Sticks

Preparation Time: 15 mins

Cooking Time: 10 mins

Servings: 3

Ingredients

- 2, large eggs
- 4 slices, thick bread
- Parchment paper
- ¼ cup, milk
- 1 tsp, cinnamon
- 1 tsp, vanilla extract
- 1 pinch, nutmeg

Steps

1. Cut each bread piece into thirds to produce the sticks. Cut a piece of parchment paper to fit the end of air fryer basin.
2. Preheat the air fryer to 360°F.
3. Combine the vanilla essence, eggs, milk, cinnamon, & nutmeg in a mixing bowl until well combined. Dip each piece of bread into to the egg mixture to ensure that it is well covered. Shake the single bread stick & place a tiny slice in the spray fryer's basket to remove excess oil. Cook several batches if necessary to avoid overcrowding the frying.
4. Fry for 4-5 minutes, then flip the bread slices and cook for another 5 minutes.

Nutritional Serving

50 Cal, Protein: 17 g, Carb: 3 g, Fat 15 g

6.8 Air-Fryer Cannoli

Preparation Time: 15 mins

Cooking Time: 10 mins

Servings: 3

Ingredients

- 1 package, milk
- ½ cup, sugar (powdered)
- 1 tbsp, orange zest
- ½ tsp, salt
- 1 cup, turbinado sugar
- Flour
- 1 package, freeze piecrusts
- 1, large egg white
- ½ cup, chocolate chips
- ½ cup, pistachios (roasted)

Steps

1. Push the ricotta through a cheesecloth-lined strainer to drain the excess liquid. Place the squeezed ricotta in a medium cup and whisk inside the salt, lime zest, & powdered sugar. The contents are spooned into a pipe vessel or a zip-top container. Wait until you're ready to use it. Place turbinado sugar on a dish. Replace the item.
2. Roll up piecrusts on a freshly floured board to 1/16-inch length. Cut 16 rectangles (3 1/2 inches) out of the

paper. Wrap cannoli molds in rings, incorporating enough egg white, so seal scraping lip. Using some of white shells, softly clean the whole covering. Roll in turbinado sugar to completely cover.

3. Apply one at a time to a loosely coated with frying oil basin approximately 3/4-inch away. Cook at 400°F for 5 to 7 minutes, or until crisp and golden. Remove with tongs and cool for about 1 minute before gently removing the cannoli form from the shell. Allow it to cool completely for about 10 minutes. Rep with the remaining shells.

4. Put chocolate chips & pistachios in separate small containers. Fill every cooled cannolo container halfway with the ricotta mixture. 1 may be dipped in chocolate or pistachio chips. Sprinkle the sugar powder over top. Serve right away.

Nutritional Serving

69 Cal, Protein: 2.8 g, Carb: 18 g, Fat 0 g

6.9 Double-Glazed Air-Fried Cinnamon Biscuit Bites

Preparation Time: 25 mins

Cooking Time: 10 mins

Servings: 4

Ingredients

- 2/3 cup, flour
- 2 tbsp, sugar
- 2/3 cup, wheat flour
- ¼ tsp, cinnamon
- 1 tsp, baking powder
- ¼ tsp, salt
- 4 tbsp, cold salted butter
- Cooking spray
- 1/3 cup, milk
- 3 tbsp, water
- 2 cups, powdered sugar

Steps

1. Whisk together the sugar, water, cinnamon, baking powder, & salt in a medium cup. Cut through the mixture with 2 blades or a pastry machine until butter is fully combined with flour & coarse cornmeal resembles mixture. Stir in the sugar until the dough forms a ball. Place dough on a floured surface & knead for 29-30 seconds, or until it is soft and has taken on a cohesive form. Separate the dough in 16 pieces. Softly roll each piece into the flat surface.

2. For cooking, spray air fryer bowl well. Spray the doughnut balls with cooking oil, spritz & place them in the basket, allowing room for each one. 11-12

minutes at 350°F until golden brown and whipped. Gently remove donut nuts from basket and place them on a wire rack over the foil. Allow 5 minutes for cooling. Rep with the remaining doughnut balls.

3. Whisk together the water & powdered sugar in a medium cup until smooth. Allow 5 minutes for cooling before glazing again, allowing the excess to drip down.

Nutritional Serving

97 Cal, Protein: 13.5 g, Carb: 0 g, Fat 7 g

6.10 Air Fryer Strawberry "Pop-Tarts"

Preparation Time: 10 mins

Cooking Time: 5 mins

Servings: 4

Ingredients

- Cooking spray
- ½ package, freeze piecrusts
- ¼ cup, sugar
- 8 ounces, strawberries
- 1 ½ tsp, lemon
- ½ cup, sugar (powdered)
- ½ ounce, candy sprinkles

Steps

1. Whisk together the sugar & strawberries in a large microwaveable dish. Allow for 15 minutes of standing time, stirring occasionally. Microwave on HIGH for about 10 minutes, or until glossy and reduced, stirring halfway through. It will take around 30 minutes to cool completely.

2. Roll out the pie dough into the 12-inch shell on a lightly floured board. Make 12 rectangles out of the dough, re-rolling scraps as needed. Spoon roughly 2 tablespoons of a strawberry mix into the center of 6 of dough rectangles, leaving a 1/2-inch margin. Brush the sides of packed dough rectangles with water, then top with remaining dough rectangles and bind with a fork. Spray the tarts generously with cooking spray.

3. Place 3 tarts inside a single layer inside an air fryer dish & bake at 350°F for 10 minutes, or until golden brown. Rep with the remaining tarts. Allow it to cool for approximately 30 minutes on a wire rack.

4. Whisk together the sugar & lemon juice inside a small cup until smooth. Glaze the cooled tarts with the spoon and liberally sprinkle with sweets.

Nutritional Serving

311 Cal, Protein: 2.8 g, Carb: 11 g, Fat 20 g

6.11 Glazed Cake Doughnut Holes

Preparation Time: 5 mins

Cooking Time: 20 mins

Servings: 2

Ingredients

- 1 ¼ cups, flour
- 2 tbsp, sugar
- Cooking spray
- 1 tsp, baking powder
- 1/3 cup, milk
- ¼ tsp, salt
- 4 tbsp, cold salted butter
- 3 tbsp, water
- 1 cup, powdered sugar

Steps

1. Whisk together the wheat, baking powder, flour, & salt in a medium mixing bowl. Add the butter and chop it into the flour with 2 forks or even a pastry cutter until it looks like gritty cornmeal. Whisk in the milk until the dough forms a ball. Knead the dough for about 30 seconds on the floured surface until it is smooth and develops a cohesive shape. Make 14 equal forms out of the dough. Roll each one gently to make consistently smooth spheres.

2. Cooking oil should fully cover bottom of a air-fryer basket. 7 dough balls should be spread evenly inside the air fryer basin to avoid striking. Spray the dough balls with the help of cooking spray. Heat at 350° F for about 10 minutes, or until golden and puffy. Remove it from the basket with care and place this on a wire shelf.

3. Whisk together the powdered sugar & water in a medium cup until smooth. 1 at a time, dip cooked dough balls in glaze and roll to coat.

4. Rep the glazing and dough-making procedure with the leftover dough.

Nutritional Serving

177 Cal, Protein: 77 g, Carb: 33 g, Fat 1.8 g

6.12 Peach Hand Pies in an Air Fryer

Preparation Time: 10 mins

Cooking Time: 25 mins

Servings: 2

Ingredients

- 3 tbsp, sugar

- 2, peaches (fresh)
- 1 tbsp, lemon
- ¼ tsp, salt
- 1 tsp, cornstarch
- 1 tsp, vanilla extract
- Cooking spray
- 1 package, freeze piecrusts

Steps

1. Combine the sugar, peaches, pepper, lemon juice, & salt in a medium cup. Allow for 15 minutes of resting time, stirring occasionally. Leave 1 tbsp of liquid after dumping the peaches. In a separate bowl, whisk together the cornstarch and the reserved liquid; pour to a peaches that were drained.

2. The piecrusts are cut into eight rounds. Fill individual circular with roughly 1 teaspoon of filling. Fold the dough over filling to make half-moons by rubbing water along the edges. To hold the pies, prick the corners with such a fork and cut three tiny slits in the tops. Spray the pies generously with frying spray.

3. Place 3 pies in an air fryer dish in a single layer & bake at 350°F for 13 to 15 minutes, or until lightly browned. Continue for the remaining pies.

Nutritional Serving

586 Cal, Protein: 37 g, Carb: 36 g, Fat 32 g

6.13 Air Fryer Churros with Chocolate Sauce

Preparation Time: 15 mins

Cooking Time: 15 mins

Servings: 12

Ingredients

- ¼ tsp, Salt
- ½ cup, Water
- 2, large Eggs
- ¼ cup, butter (Non-salted)
- ½ cup, Flour
- 2 tsp, Cinnamon
- 1/3 cup, Sugar
- 4 ounces, Chocolate chips
- 2 tbsp, Vanilla kefir
- 3 tbsp, Cream

Steps

1. In a small saucepan, bring the sugar, salt, and 1/4 cup butter to a boil over medium-high heat. Reduce the heat to low and stir in the flour with such a wooden spoon for about 30 seconds, or till the dough becomes smooth. Cook for another 2 to 3 minutes, constantly stirring, until the

dough begins to pull away from the edges of the pan and a film forms on the bottom of plate. In a medium plate, place the dough. Stir constantly for about 1 minute or until the mixture has somewhat cooled. 1 egg at a time, constantly whisking after each addition until smooth. Transfer the solution to a pipe container with a medium star tip. Chill for thirty minutes.

2. In an air fryer basket, pipe 6 single-layer pieces. At 380° F, cook until crispy, about 10 minutes. Rep with the remaining dough.

3. Whisk together the sugar & cinnamon in a medium mixing bowl. Brush the remaining 2 tbsp of melted butter over the cooked churros before covering them with sugar mixture.

4. In a small microwave-safe dish, combine the cream and chocolate. Microwave for 30 seconds on HIGH, or until melted and flat, rotating after 14 seconds. Stir in the kefir. Garnish the churros with such a chocolate sauce.

Nutritional Serving

147 Cal, Protein: 2 g, Carb: 20 g, Fat 6 g

6.14 Chocolate Orange Christmas Biscuits

Preparation Time: 5 mins

Cooking Time: 10 mins

Servings: 4

Ingredients

- 225 g, flour
- 100 g, sugar
- 100 g, butter
- 1, large orange juice
- 1, egg large
- 2 tbsp, cocoa powder
- 2 tsp, vanilla essence
- dark chocolate

Steps

1. Preheat the air fryer to 180 degrees Celsius.
2. In a mixing basin, combine the flour & butter and knead the fat until the mixture resembles breadcrumbs.
3. Blend in the cinnamon, spice, orange, and cocoa powder until smooth.
4. Blend in your egg until the dough is just a bit sticky and resembles the mixture.
5. Make 8 equal-sized dough balls by sprinkling flour on your hands to prevent the mixture from sticking to you.
6. Flatten dough balls & place a square of dark chocolate into each slice, then cover it with dough to hide the chocolate.
7. I cooked all 8 parts for 15 minutes at 180°C in an air fryer.
8. It's just for serving.

Nutritional Serving

147 Cal, Protein: 2 g, Carb: 20 g, Fat 6 g

6.15 Air fryer Oat Sandwich Biscuits

Preparation Time: 35 mins

Cooking Time: 15 mins

Servings: 5

Ingredients

- 150 g, flour
- 100 g, butter
- 75 g, white sugar
- ½, small egg
- ¼ cup, coconut
- ½ cup, gluten-free oats
- 20 g, white chocolate
- 1 tsp, vanilla essence

Steps

1. Cream the sugar & butter together until light and creamy. Add chocolate, mint, & coconut to the recipe's nature. Blend in the flour well.
2. Make medium-sized biscuit shapes, then roll them in oats.
3. Preheat the air fryer to 180°C and cook for 17 minutes.
4. While they're cooling, make the filling. Mix the butter & icing sugar together until a frothy mixture is formed. Mix in lemon juice & vanilla extract, then blend again and place on one hand.
5. Whereas the biscuits are still cold, spread the filling on them & press them together to make a delicious sandwich.

Nutritional Serving

141 Cal, Protein: 5 g, Carb: 13 g, Fat 7 g

6.16 Half Cooked Air Fryer Lemon Biscuits

Preparation Time: 35 mins

Cooking Time: 15 mins

Servings: 10

Ingredients

- 100 g, butter
- 100 g, sugar
- 225 g, flour
- 1, small lemon
- 1, small egg
- 1 tsp, vanilla essence

Steps

1. Preheat your air fryer to 180 degrees Celsius.

2. In a mixing basin, combine the sugar and flour. Rub the butter into the mixture until it resembles breadcrumbs. Shake the cup sufficiently to get the fatty bits to fall to surface.

3. Combine the egg & lemon juice in a mixing bowl.

4. Incorporate and mix until you have a wonderful fluffy bread.

5. Stretch the dough out and cut it into medium-sized biscuits.

6. Place the biscuits on a baking pan in the air fryer & bake for 5 mins at 180°C.

7. Place on a cooling sheet & dust with icing sugar.

Nutritional Serving

135 Cal, Protein: 7 g, Carb: 9 g, Fat 8 g

6.17 Melting Moments in Air fryer

Preparation Time: 10 mins

Cooking Time: 5 mins

Servings: 2

Ingredients

- 100 g, butter
- 75 g, sugar
- 150 g, flour
- 1 small, egg
- 50 g, white chocolate
- 3 tbsp, coconut
- 1 tsp, vanilla essence

Steps

1. Preheat the air fryer to 180 degrees Fahrenheit.

2. Cream the sugar & butter together in a large mixing bowl until light and creamy.

3. The vanilla flavor is added once the eggs have been smashed.

4. Use a roller pin to combine the large and small pieces of white chocolate.

5. Blend in the flour and white chocolate until smooth.

6. Roll the coconut into little balls & cover them.

7. Put the balls on a baking sheet inside the air fryer & bake for eight minutes at 180 degrees Celsius. Reduce the temperature to 160°C for another 4 minutes.

8. Simply put, serve.

Nutritional Serving

96 Cal, Protein: 4 g, Carb: 2 g, Fat 8 g

6.18 Air Fryer Shortbread

Preparation Time: 35 mins

Cooking Time: 15 mins

Servings: 4

Ingredients

- 250 g, Flour
- 75 g, Sugar
- 175 g, Butter

Steps

1. In a cup, combine the self-raised flour, butter, & caster sugar.
2. In the starch, rub the butter until it resembles thick breadcrumbs.
3. Marinate, & you'll have a shortbread dough ball.
4. Using cookie cutters, cut into your desired shapes.
5. Shortbread should be fried in an air fryer on one of the air freezer grill pans. Set the timer for 10 minutes at 181 degrees Celsius/360 degrees Fahrenheit.
6. Allow it to cool somewhat before serving.

Nutritional Serving

180 Cal, Protein: 15 g, Carb: 1 g, Fat 13 g

6.19 Air Fryer Cupcakes

Preparation Time: 25 mins

Cooking Time: 10 mins

Servings: 12

Ingredients

- 400 g, flour
- 450 g, sugar
- 50 g, cocoa powder
- 200 g, butter
- 4 mediums, eggs
- 1 tbsp, vanilla essence
- 480 ml, milk
- 1 tbsp, olive oil (extra virgin)

Steps

1. In a mixing bowl, combine the butter and sugar. Using a hand mixer, incorporate the butter into sugar. In a cup, crack an egg, add the vanilla essence, extra virgin olive oil, & mix with a hand blender once more. With a wooden spoon, mix inside cocoa powder, flour, & milk if it's frothy. A hand mixer should not be used since it has the potential to spill everything. If it's too thick, thin it up with a bit more milk or water.
2. Fill muffin cups halfway with batter and bake for 12 minutes at 160°C/320°F in an air fryer. Set it aside to cool on one side.
3. As the chocolate buttercream cools, prepare it. Using a hand mixer, whisk the icing sugar in the butter. Connect a few components and mix them together till you get a smooth buttercream. Refrigerate the cupcakes after they have cooled.

4. Using your piping bag, make a fist from the rear. Then open your palm over it, creating a funnel shape. Then, using your other hand, pour the mixture in the piping container.

5. When the top of piping bag is nearly entirely grabbed and twisted closed, gently press down and swirl it on top to enable the air to escape.

Nutritional Serving

38 Cal, Protein: 1 g, Carb: 5 g, Fat 1 g

6.20 Air Fryer Lemon Butterfly Buns

Preparation Time: 20 mins

Cooking Time: 15 mins

Servings: 5

Ingredients

- 100 g, butter
- 100 g, sugar
- 2, medium eggs
- 100 g, flour
- ½ tsp, vanilla essence
- 1 tsp, cherries
- 50 g, butter
- 100 g, icing sugar
- ½, small lemon juice

Steps

1. Preheat an air fryer to 170 degrees Fahrenheit.
2. Cream the butter and honey together in a large mixing basin until light and fluffy.
3. Include the definition of Vanilla.
4. Make sure each egg provides a little amount of starch by beating them together.
5. Pull the rest of the flour in with care.
6. Before you run out of containers, cover half of the mixture with the little bun casings. Place the very first six in Air fryer & cook for 8 minutes at 170°C.
7. Because the buns were baking, begin preparing the icing sugar. Cream the butter & gradually add the icing sugar. Blend in the lemon until it is completely smooth. If it's too thick, add a little water.
8. When butterfly buns were completely baked, remove the top slice off the buns, cut in two, and create butterfly shapes. Place the icing sugar in middle of the cake. Then sprinkle tiny bit icing sugar on the top of 1/3 of the cherry.
9. Simply put, serve.

Nutritional Serving

706 Cal, Protein: 35 g, Carb: 44 g, Fat 42 g

6.21 Air Fryer Apple Crisp

Preparation Time: 30 mins

Cooking Time: 10 mins

Servings: 12

Ingredients

- 6, Medium Apples
- 1 Tbsp, Sugar
- 1 Tbsp, Cinnamon
- 120 g, Flour
- 40 g, Sugar
- 50 g, Butter
- 60 g, Oats

Steps

1. Put the apples in a mixing dish after peeling and dicing them. In a mixing bowl, combine the sugar & cinnamon from caster sugar. Make your way to Ramekins.
2. Stack the flour & butter in a cup and stir the fat into flour till coarse breadcrumbs form.
3. Combine. When it's completely mixed, add the sugar and oats.
4. Cover. Toss the apples with the topping and set the ramekins in the air fryer basket.
5. All you have to do is cook. Start with 8 minutes at 160°F/320°F, then 5 minutes at 200°F/400°F, and serve.

Nutritional Serving

49 Cal, Protein: 3 g, Carb: 4 g, Fat 2 g

6.22 Chocolate Mug Cake

Preparation Time: 20 mins

Cooking Time: 10 mins

Servings: 10

Ingredients

- ¼ Cup, Flour
- 5 Tbsp, Sugar
- 1 Tbsp, Cocoa Powder
- 3 Tbsp, Milk
- 3 Tsp, Coconut Oil

Steps

1. In a cup, thoroughly mix all of the ingredients. But make sure they're well mixed, otherwise, you'll end up with a cake with hardly any chocolate & then have to fill the next one.
2. Refrigerate the cup and bake at 200°C for 10 minutes. Rinse and repeat with the remaining cups until everyone has gotten their chocolate fix.
3. It should be served.

Nutritional Serving

200 Cal, Protein: 6 g, Carb: 2 g, Fat 6 g

6.23 Air Fryer Blueberry Jam Tarts

Preparation Time: 20 mins

Cooking Time: 10 mins

Servings: 6

Ingredients

- 350 g, Pie crust
- 500 g, Blueberry Jam

Steps

1. Flour tart tins to keep the pastry from sticking together.
2. Roll out the pie crust on a work surface and put it over the tart pans.
3. Break the tart pans around them to make a pie crust with each one.
4. Fill your tarts to the tops with blueberry jam.
5. Cook for 10 minutes in a fryer oven basket at 180°C/360°F.
6. It's just for serving.

Nutritional Serving

160 Cal, Protein: 4 g, Carb: 3 g, Fat 13 g

6.24 Chocolate Orange Chocolate Fondant

Preparation Time: 20 mins

Cooking Time: 10 mins

Servings: 4

Ingredients

- 2 tbsp, flour
- 4 tbsp, sugar
- 115 g, dark chocolate
- 115 g, butter
- 1 medium, orange
- 2 medium, eggs

Steps

1. Preheat the oven to 200 degrees Fahrenheit and the refrigerator to 180 degrees Fahrenheit.
2. Melt the butter & chocolate in a glass dish over a large pan of boiling water. Stir the color until it is smooth & creamy.
3. Whisk and pound the eggs & sugar until they are bright and foamy.
4. Connect the orange, as well as the egg & sugar mixture to the chocolate. Finally, mix in the flour until everything is fully combined.
5. Fill the ramekins % full with the mixture & bake approximately 11 minutes.

6. Remove the ramekins from the fridge & cook for 2 mins in the ramekins. Turn the ramekins upside down on such a serving platter and massage the bottoms with such a blunt blade to release the tips.

7. You'll get a gorgeous pudding with such a fluffy core after releasing the fondant from center.

8. Serve over ice cream or a hot milk syrup.

Nutritional Serving

357 Cal, Protein: 15 g, Carb: 55 g, Fat 10 g

6.25 Air Fryer Pumpkin Pie

Preparation Time: 30 mins

Cooking Time: 15 mins

Servings: 6

Ingredients

- 225 g, flour
- 100 g, butter
- 25 g, sugar
- 1 tbsp, cinnamon
- 1 tsp, nutmeg

Steps

1. Get the sandwich's customary crust. In a bowl, combine the cut butter and flour until it resembles breadcrumbs. Combine the cinnamon, sugar, & nutmeg in a mixing bowl. Blend in a little amount of water at a time till you have a smooth pie crust. Remove the pie crust and place it in pie pan.

2. 1 cup water, 1 cup pumpkin, 1 cup ginger, 1 cup pumpkin, 1 cup ginger, 1 cup water, 1 cup water, 1 cup water, 1 cup water, 1 cup water Under manual pressure/pressure, cook for 4 minutes. Use manual pressure release and rapid pressure release.

3. Instantly clean your pot. Using a strainer, drain the liquid from your Instant Pot & then rinse this with a milky cloth. Because the pumpkin has a number, any excess liquid may be removed, as it will disrupt the arrangement of your pumpkin pie if you don't.

4. Create a pumpkin pie topping. Return the cleaned pumpkin and ginger to the Instant Cup and stir in all of the pumpkin-filled ingredients except the milk. Using a hand mixer, beat the eggs and additional ingredients into pumpkin until you get a creamy, rich pumpkin sauce. In the double milk, whisk and combine well.

5. Put the pie filling in a pie crust, ensuring it does not extend more than 1 cm over the edge since it would be difficult to control and likely to bubble over.

6. Cook the pumpkin pie in an air fryer. Bake the pumpkin pie for 24 minutes at 180°C/360°F on the middle shelf.

7. Place it in the refrigerator and let it to chill overnight. The pumpkin pie will harden up as a result, and it'll be ready to slice the following day.

Nutritional Serving

90 Cal, Protein: 6 g, Carb: 10 g, Fat 3 g

6.26 Leftover Coconut Sugar Recipes

Preparation Time: 25 mins

Cooking Time: 15 mins

Servings: 4

Ingredients

- 500 g, flour
- 350 g, butter
- 100 g, cheese
- 200 g, coconut sugar
- 2 tbsp, honey
- 1 tsp, vanilla essence
- 1 tsp, cinnamon

Steps

1. Preheat the air fryer to 180 degrees Fahrenheit.
2. In a mixing bowl, combine the rice, butter, & sugar. Using the rubbing method, work the fat into the flour & sugar till it resembles breadcrumbs.
3. Continue baking until a smooth dough appears after adding the cinnamon and honey.
4. Divide it into three halves. 1/5 on a work surface for the next use, 2/5 in a bowl for the center, and the leftover 2/2 for covering.
5. Place a baking mat in bottom of the air fryer.
6. Line the bottom of an air fryer with a very light coating of dough (using your fingers instead of a rolling pin) to create a cheesecake rim.
7. Cook for five min at 180°C with the fryer suspended in the air.
8. Set the air fryer at a height of one foot. While the puff pastry is chilling, make the fluffy filling. In a mixing bowl, combine the cheese and 2/5 of the dough till you get a beautiful cheesecake-style mixture that is richer than a regular cheesecake yet light and fluffy. In the air fryer, combine the blackberries and place them on top of crust.
9. Spread that on top of the shortbread cheesecake spread with your hands so that it may take the form of your top crumble.
10. Preheat the air fryer to 180 degrees Fahrenheit for 15 minutes. Cook until you're on top of a lovely crumble.

11. Remove shortbread strips from air fryer & arrange them on a broad dish in the fridge so that the cheesecake may be fully placed in the middle.
12. Serve by cutting into bars.

Nutritional Serving

151 Cal, Protein: 5 g, Carb: 31 g, Fat 3 g

6.27 Air Fryer Mince Pies

Preparation Time: 30 mins

Cooking Time: 10 mins

Servings: 6

Ingredients

- 500 g, pie crust
- 350 g, jar mincemeat
- 1, small egg
- 50 g, icing sugar
- flour

Steps

1. Combine the pie ingredients in a mixing basin. Stir in the sugar after rubbing the flour with grease. Even if you've a pastry with some water, add a little extra virgin olive oil & combine.
2. Flour a roller pin as well as a clean work surface. Using pastry cutters, roll out the pastry & cut it out to the appropriate size.
3. Fill muffin tins halfway with dough and top with a spoonful of minced meat.
4. Apply another piece of pastry over top, pressing down and covering with your hands to ensure that no thin flesh escapes throughout the process.
5. Apply an egg coating to the surface of your thin pies with a pastry brush before placing them in the air fryer. Cook for 14 mins at 180°C/360°F in your air fryer oven.
6. Eat right now or store for later. A sprinkling of icing sugar around the pies is also a nice touch.

Nutritional Serving

413 Cal, Protein: 39 g, Carb: 21 g, Fat 20 g

6.28 Air Fryer Brownies

Preparation Time: 25 mins

Cooking Time: 20 mins

Servings: 4

Ingredients

- 100 g, flour
- 100 g, butter
- 2, large eggs

- 30 g, cocoa powder
- 175 g, brown sugar
- 1 tbsp, golden syrup
- 2 tsp, vanilla essence

Steps

1. Fill the air fryer's baking pan with butter and split it up into bite-size pieces. Place the baking pan in air fryer's basket & cook for 2 minutes at 140°C/280°F, or until the cheese has melted.
2. It cools down enough when you can touch it.
3. Fill your fryer baking pan with sugar, eggs, golden syrup, cocoa powder, & vanilla extract. With the whisk on your hand, thoroughly combine the ingredients.
4. Mix in the flour with a fork till everything is well combined.
5. Place the baking pan in air fryer bowl & cook for 14 mins at 180°C/360°F, or until a cocktail thread inserted in the center of the brownies comes out clean.
6. Serve over whipped cream, caramel sauce, and any other desired toppings.

Nutritional Serving

528 Cal, Protein: 11 g, Carb: 97 g, Fat 11 g

6.29 Chocolate Eclairs in The Air Fryer

Preparation Time: 15 mins

Cooking Time: 20 mins

Servings: 6

Ingredients

- 50 g, butter
- 100 g, flour
- 3, medium eggs
- 150 ml, water

Steps

1. Preheat an air fryer to 180 degrees Fahrenheit.
2. While the water is heating up, put the fat in a large pan and melt it over medium heat, then raise it to a boil.
3. Remove this from the heat & add the flour, whisking constantly.
4. Return the pan to a heat & swirl to form a medium disc in the middle.
5. Once eggs are combined, transfer the dough to the cold dish to chill till you have a beautiful combination.
6. Then render and shape into éclairs in the Air fryer. Cook for 10 minutes at 180°F, then for another 8 minutes at 160°F.
7. While the dough is baking, make cream filling by whisking together the vanilla

extract, icing sugar, & whipped cream till smooth and thick.

Nutritional Serving

174 Cal, Protein: 10 g, Carb: 12 g, Fat 9 g

6.30 Air Fryer Chocolate Profiteroles

Preparation Time: 10 mins

Cooking Time: 10 mins

Servings: 3

Ingredients

- 100 g, butter
- 200 g, flour
- 6, medium eggs
- 300 ml, water

Steps

1. Preheat an air fryer to 170 degrees Fahrenheit.
2. Put your fat in a large pan with water and heat on medium to ensure it comes to a boil.
3. Remove it from the heat & stir in the flour, then return it to the heat till it forms a big dough in the middle of the dish.
4. To cool down the dough, adjust it from one side. Add the eggs and combine until you have a lovely mixture.
5. Make profiterole shapes & bake at 180°C for 8-10 minutes.
6. When creating the eclairs, whisk together the cream filling, vanilla extract, icing sugar, and whipped cream till thick and heavy.
7. Make the chocolate coating whereas the profiteroles are frying by combining the chocolate, cream, & butter in a glass cup set more than a pan of boiling water. Before you have melted chocolate, mix everything together.
8. Finish the dark chocolate profiteroles on the outside.

Nutritional Serving

373 Cal, Protein: 17 g, Carb: 45 g, Fat 13 g

6.31 Air Fryer Doughnuts from Scratch

Preparation Time: 20 mins

Cooking Time: 10 mins

Servings: 4

Ingredients

- 500 g, doughnut dough (bread maker)
- 240 ml, icing sugar
- 40 ml, milk
- 1 tsp, vanilla essence
- olive oil spray (extra virgin)

- flour for rolling
- food coloring

Steps

1. Remove the doughnut dough from the bread machine and place it on a floured surface. Add flour to prevent it from sticking.
2. Use your biscuit cutters to cut out the huge doughnut shapes. Using a smaller knife, cut out doughnut holes. To one hand, put the holes in doughnut.
3. All you have to do is cook. Fill the air fryer basket with up to 4 doughnuts and cook for 8 minutes at 180°C/360°F. After 4 minutes, spritz with olive oil to aid with the delicate glow.
4. Terminate. Combine the icing sugar & milk in a cup to make a thick glaze. Apply food coloring to the doughnuts or break them into ramekins to make different colored doughnuts. With the 100's & 1000's, sprinkle and eat.

Nutritional Serving

164 Cal, Protein: 5 g, Carb: 15 g, Fat 11 g

6.32 Air Fryer Baking for Easter

Preparation Time: 25 mins

Cooking Time: 15 mins

Servings: 8

Ingredients

- 225 g, milk chocolate
- 50 g, butter
- 75 g, corn
- 1 tbsp, golden syrup
- 200 g, Cadbury's mini eggs

Steps

1. Break the dairy milk into squares & place them on the fryer baking pan with butter & golden syrup. Cook for 5 minutes at 140°C/280°F, stirring constantly until the butter & chocolate have fully melted and mixed. Before all of the breakfast cereals are coated in chocolate, add them and combine thoroughly. In the baking cups, place a few small eggs in a bowl of the each cake and refrigerate. After an hour, take it out of the fridge and feed it.
2. Next, prepare the cake batter. In a mixing bowl, cream together the butter and sugar with such a hand mixer till smooth & fluffy. Add the eggs & whisk again on low, then whisk in the other ingredients inside the cake batter and incorporate well with a fork. Fill silicone cupcake liners or similar containers halfway with cake batter and place inside the air fryer basket. Cook for 10 minutes at

180°C/360°F. Remove the air fryer from the heat and set aside to cool.

3. Render the cupcake icing while the cupcakes are cooling. In a cup, combine the icing sugar with the cream cheese and mix again with your hand blender. The vanilla essence is poured to icing sugar lumps & gently mixed with a fork after it's smooth and fluffy.

4. While the cupcake icing is still cool, it is filled. Wait till the cakes have reached room temp before sprinkling the cupcake icing on top. Attach the small chickens and feed them.

Nutritional Serving

258 Cal, Protein: 19 g, Carb: 19 g, Fat 11 g

6.33 Molten lava cake

Preparation Time: 20 mins

Cooking Time: 15 mins

Servings: 4

Ingredients

- 1, egg yolk
- 1, egg
- 2 tbsp, unsalted butter
- 3 tbsp, white caster sugar
- ½ tbsp, vanilla extract
- 3 tbsp, flour
- 30 g, chocolate
- 1 pinch, salt

Steps

1. Whisk together vanilla extract, butter, and sugar in a large mixing bowl until the mixture is smooth and fluffy.

2. In a mixing bowl, whisk together the egg yolk and whites, then add to the butter and sugar mixture. Whisk until the mixture has a creamy consistency.

3. Add the flour & salt to a mixture stir it in with a spatula.

4. Heat the chocolate in the microwave for about a minute or until melted, then add it to the mixture and mix thoroughly.

5. Fill a greased ramekin and similar air-freezer-safe vessel halfway with this mixture.

6. Place the bowls in a fryer at 180° C for 8-10 minutes.

Nutritional Serving

676 Cal, Protein: 24 g, Carb: 60 g, Fat 36 g

6.34 Basque Burnt Cheesecake

Preparation Time: 50 mins

Cooking Time: 10 mins

Servings: 13

Ingredients

- 250 g, cheese
- 1, egg yolk
- 2, eggs
- 70 g, sugar
- 0.5 g, vanilla extract
- 170 g, whipping cream
- 6 g, cake flour

Steps

1. Preheat the air fryer to 200 degrees Celsius.
2. Using a blender or whisk, combine the cream cheese and sugar.
3. Blend in the egg yolks and entire eggs in small batches till the liquid has a wet, soupy texture.
4. Mix in the milk & vanilla essence from the whipping cream until everything is well combined.
5. In a separate bowl, sift your cake flour & whisk till smooth.
6. Line a pan with nonstick baking paper and pour the ingredients in.
7. Bake at 180°C for 18 minutes, then at 200°C for another 3-5 minutes, or until the cake top is black.
8. Serve refrigerated or at room temperature.

Nutritional Serving

127 Cal, Protein: 6 g, Carb: 10 g, Fat 7 g

6.35 Banana Muffin

Preparation Time: 15 mins

Cooking Time: 15 mins

Servings: 12

Ingredients

- 2, bananas
- ⅓ cup, olive oil
- 1, egg
- ½ cup, sugar
- 1 tsp, vanilla extract
- 1 tsp, cinnamon
- ¾ cup, flour

Steps

1. In a large mixing bowl, mash the bananas, then add the vanilla essence, sugar, bacon, & olive oil. Mix thoroughly.
2. Fold in the cinnamon & flour until the batter is well combined.
3. Distribute the batter evenly among the muffin tins.
4. Place this in a hot air fryer set to 160° C for approximately 15 minutes.

Nutritional Serving

80 Cal, Protein: 3 g, Carb: 16 g, Fat 1

Conclusion

By many measures, air frying is better than frying in just oil. It lessens calories by 70-80% & has very less or no fat. This cooking method may also reduce other impacts of oil frying. If you're looking to trim the waistline, swapping the deep-fried cooking with air-fried cooking could be a very nice idea. Study on the effects of air-fried food is presently limited, but experts advise that we shall cut down on the intake of fried food regardless of the cooking mode. Just because the food is air-fried doesn't mean it is healthful. Try to integrate other cooking options also in the diets, such as roasting, baking, grilling, & pan-searing foods. Preserving a variety of cooking approaches & foods will assist you in staying fit & maintain a strong lifestyle.

Though, as the air fryers fry different foods, you cannot cook every food in the air fryer. Diabetes, high blood pressure, heart syndromes, and specific cancers are ascribed to fried foods. For normal meals, restricting fried foods and concentrating on stable cooking methods like steaming, roasting and sauteing is best. Even still, not just can the air fryer make items that you would typically deep-fry. It can also make any food you usually cook on your stove or microwave. It's a fantastic way to heat foods with no rubbery, & it is a fabulous & swift way to cook & make meals with different ingredients. In present years, it's the best new kitchen appliance that has been revealed.

In the end, the conclusion is that it is an attractive, slick appliance. It could fulfill all the needs of eating all the lip-spanking & delicious fried food with no or little oil. The consequences are so much healthier than oil frying, and your kitchen also becomes mess-free too. While it also does an admirable job heating other meats & vegetables, the air fryer truly shines at fake deep frying.

Printed in Great Britain
by Amazon